WHEN KINGS
PRAY&
FAST

WHEN KINGS
PRAY&
FAST

H.R.M.
KING ADAMTEY I

WHITAKER
HOUSE

Unless otherwise indicated, all Scripture quotations are taken from the *Holy Bible, New International Version*®, © 1973, 1978, 1984 by the International Bible Society. Used by permission of Zondervan. All rights reserved. Scripture quotations marked (KJV) are taken from the King James Version of the Holy Bible.

The information presented here is not intended as medical advice. Always consult your physician before undertaking any change in your physical regimen, whether fasting, diet, or exercise.

WHEN KINGS PRAY AND FAST
Based on the text of *Prayer and Fasting* by Dr. Kingsley Fletcher

Dr. Kingsley A. Fletcher
PO Box 12017
Research Triangle Park, NC 27709-2017

ISBN-13: 978-0-88368-181-7
ISBN-10: 0-88368-181-1
Printed in the United States of America
© 1992, 2006 by Dr. Kingsley A. Fletcher

1030 Hunt Valley Circle
New Kensington, PA 15068
www.whitakerhouse.com

Library of Congress Cataloging-in-Publication Data
Fletcher, Kingsley A.
When kings pray and fast / by Kingsley A. Fletcher.
p. cm.
Summary: "Outlines principles for effective fasting while examining the role of fasting in the prayer lives of Christians"—Provided by publisher.
"Based on the text of Prayer & fasting by Dr. Kingsley A. Fletcher"—ECIP t.p. verso.
ISBN-13: 978-0-88368-181-7 (trade pbk. : alk. paper)
ISBN-10: 0-88368-181-1 (trade pbk. : alk. paper)
1. Prayer—Christianity. 2. Fasting—Religious aspects—Christianity. 3. Prayer—Biblical teaching. 4. Fasting—Biblical teaching. I. Fletcher, Kingsley A. Prayer & fasting. II. Title.
BV210.3.F57 2005
248.4'7—dc22   2005017423

1 2 3 4 5 6 7 8 9 10 11 12 ⨆⨆ 14 13 12 11 10 09 08 07 06

ACKNOWLEDGMENTS

I am eternally grateful for my father, who is deceased, and my mother for the leadership, investment, and training they provided me. Their wealth of wisdom and knowledge continues to produce in my life to this very day.

Finally, I want to recognize the numerous unknown heroes who have touched the world by sacrificing their lives to further the kingdom of God.

CONTENTS

Introduction

MATTHEW 17:14–21 KJV

And when they were come to the multitude, there came to him a certain man, kneeling down to him, and saying, Lord, have mercy on my son: for he is a lunatic, and sore vexed: for ofttimes he falleth into the fire, and oft into the water. And I brought him to thy disciples, and they could not cure him. Then Jesus answered and said, O faithless and perverse generation, how long shall I be with you? how long shall I suffer you? bring him hither to me. And Jesus rebuked the devil; and he departed out of him: and the child was cured from that very hour. Then came the disciples to Jesus apart, and said, Why could not we cast him out? And Jesus said unto them, Because of your unbelief: for verily I say unto you, If ye have faith as a grain of mustard seed, ye shall say unto this mountain, Remove hence to yonder place; and it shall remove; and nothing shall be impossible unto you. Howbeit this kind goeth not out but by prayer and fasting.

INTRODUCTION

I am convinced that one of the reasons today's church is so frequently powerless is that it has lost sight of the godly custom of prayer and fasting. It has succumbed to the sins of gluttony, selfishness, and pride. Yet, now more than ever, the church needs to be its strongest as the enemy rails against us in these final days.

Scripture reveals over and over that prayer and fasting is a central key to our strength and deliverance:

> *There came to him a certain man, kneeling down to him, and saying, Lord, have mercy on my son: for he is a lunatic, and sore vexed: for ofttimes he falleth into the fire, and oft into the water. And I brought him to thy disciples, and they could not cure him....And Jesus rebuked the devil; and he departed out of him: and the child was cured from that very hour.*
>
> (Matthew 17:14–16, 18 KJV)

When Jesus drove out the demon that had so vexed the disciples, they turned to Him with a very logical question: "Why couldn't we do that? Why couldn't we heal the boy? What's your secret?" As always, Jesus' response cut to the chase:

> *This kind goeth not out but by prayer and fasting.*
>
> (verse 21 KJV)

11

WHEN KINGS PRAY AND FAST

The type of miracle needed by this man and his son cannot be realized by people who are self-centered in prayer and undisciplined in fasting. Only those who are willing to learn how to pray and fast effectively and to fervently seek the face of God will experience the power of God in their lives.

There is another truth that many Christians seem to have lost sight of that (combined with the immense power of prayer and fasting) makes us virtually undefeatable: We are royalty!

You are a chosen people, a royal priesthood, a holy nation, a people belonging to God, that you may declare the praises of him who called you out of darkness into his wonderful light.

(1 Peter 2:9)

In these final days, people have allowed themselves to become distracted by the daily challenges of life. But we all face challenges, no matter what our roles in society, and we shouldn't allow them to stop us from marching into what God has for us. This is particularly true of people in positions of great authority. In fact, the higher the position, the more responsibility a leader has to mobilize his people into a unified effort to resolve life's challenges. This is never truer than when opposition and trials come our way.

It is during difficult times that opportunity arises to unite people with one another and with God. When faced with situations concerning the welfare of their people, many great kings and leaders throughout history have galvanized their people to come together to seek the face of God for direction. The same is true for each one of us: The Word of God tells us that we have been raised into royal positions of kings and priests to be in heavenly places with Jesus Christ. That authorizes us—indeed, compels us—to carry out His commands upon this earth! It is in that light that we need to begin to see ourselves, for we have been chosen for positions of leadership.

INTRODUCTION

The Spirit itself beareth witness with our spirit, that we are the children of God: and if children, then heirs; heirs of God, and joint-heirs with Christ; if so be that we suffer with him, that we may be also glorified together. (Romans 8:16–17 KJV)

As joint heirs with Christ Jesus, we bear the power and authority of the King. As such, we must begin to think with a kingdom mentality in order to approach God's throne with confidence. It is necessary to come together at times to pray and fast as a people. Kings must encourage corporate prayer and fasting, the combined submission of all the people to God's will and plan.

Recently, an article appeared in the *London Times* in which Michael Gove examined how political leaders learn when they submit themselves to God: "Christian faith helps leaders gain a frame of reference for their decisions beyond that of mere political expediency. Far from becoming arrogant, inflexible, and intolerant, Christian leaders are forced to face the fact that they are answerable to a higher authority."[1]

Commenting on Michael Gove's article, Chris Armstrong said,

> Though non-Christians, too, have shown such enlightened compassion in their leadership, Gove's challenge reminds us that Christian leadership has been the norm—not the exception—for most of Western history. And despite the decidedly mixed record of such leadership, examples abound—from Constantine, Theodosius I, and Justinian I through Charlemagne, Louis IX, and Elizabeth I—of rulers who have taken seriously the faith they professed and allowed it to influence their policies to the benefit of their people.[2]

---

[1] Michael Gove, *London Times* article paraphrased by Chris Armstrong, "When World Leaders Pray," <http://www.christianitytoday.com/history/newsletter/2003/may16.html> (7 June 2005).

[2] Chris Armstrong, "When World Leaders Pray," <http://www.christianitytoday.com/history/newsletter/2003/may16.html> (7 June 2005).

WHEN KINGS PRAY AND FAST

The royal career of England's Elizabeth I (1533–1603) radiates with a combination of strong, active faith and prudent, sensitive rulership. A portion of a prayer she authored in 1574 reads:

> And that as I do acknowledge to have received the Government of this Church and Kingdome at Thy hand, and to hold the same of Thee, so graunt me grace, O Lord, that in the end I may render up and present the same unto Thee, a peaceable, quiet, and well ordered State and Kingdome, as also a perfect reformed Church, to the furtherance of Thy Glory. And to my subjects, O Lord God, graunt, I beseech Thee, faithfull and obedient hearts, willingly to submit themselves to the obedience of Thy Word and Commandments, that we altogether being thankfull unto Thee for Thy benefitts received, may laud and magnifie Thy Holy Name world without end. Graunt this, O mercifull Father, for Jesus Christes sake our only Mediatour and Advocate. Amen.[3]

One of the challenges faced by many contemporary democratic societies is that they don't fully understand "kingdoms." This is due to their lack of living under the authority of a king. In a democratic society, rule is by majority vote. In a kingdom, only one person is in charge: The king is the sole ruling authority. He sets the agenda for the nation, oversees the protection and betterment of the citizens, leads and guides them in matters both great and small, and renders and executes judgment—which a righteous king will do with grace and mercy.

As a king and a leader of the Shai kingdom in the African state of Ghana, I regularly summon the people to pray and fast. Recently, leaders and citizens of the Shai kingdom, along with representatives of various churches and agencies throughout Ghana, joined together to seek God concerning several areas of need:

---

[3] Chris Armstrong, "When World Leaders Pray, Part II," <http://www.christianitytoday.com/history/newsletter/2003/may30.html> (7 June 2005).

INTRODUCTION

- God's favor and prosperity upon the Shai people
- His blessings upon all the divisional kings, queens and mothers, the royals, the traditional leadership, and all the subjects of the kingdom
- Healing for our land
- Physical healing for our people
- The breaking of strongholds that affect our entire kingdom
- Business opportunities for the Shai State and its people
- True unity to prevail in all our endeavors

That was a life-changing event for the Shai state—and we experienced phenomenal answers from God! As a result of His miraculous responses, I directed that prayer meetings shall take place throughout the kingdom on a regular basis. The consequences of our coming together to acknowledge God as our one true King and Leader, and seeking Him for answers to the challenges we were facing, proved that, when kings pray and fast, God answers!

> *If my people, who are called by my name, will humble themselves and pray and seek my face and turn from their wicked ways, then will I hear from heaven and will forgive their sin and will heal their land.* (2 Chronicles 7:14)

As a king in two realms (the heavenly inheritance all believers are called to, and my earthly responsibilities as a king of the Shai people), I embrace my responsibility not only to call the people to pray and fast, but also to teach them the proper way to do so.

My hope is that, in reading this book, you will be encouraged to reach out to God in consistent prayer and fasting, and to seek Him continually for guidance and direction in your life, in the knowledge that you, too, are being raised up as a king. If we are to experience mighty revival in these days, and if we are to put down the kingdom of Satan and see the power of God fully prevail, then we must learn to crucify our flesh so that our spirit-man can commune in liberty with our heavenly Father. The only way that can be accomplished with power is through prayer and fasting.

May God fire up your spirit to the loftiest heights of His mighty kingdom as you learn these practical methods for effective prayer and fasting. Many of your most challenging problems can be solved by returning to this biblical practice. If you are seeking kingdom results in your life, then you need to exercise kingly principles, for God is raising up a Royal Priesthood to reign in power and authority over the whole earth!

So come with me now, and let us discover as joint heirs with Christ how God's awesome power and presence is manifested when kings pray and fast....

—His Royal Majesty KING ADAMTEY I
SE SUAPOLOR
Ghana, West Africa
Peace, Progress, Prosperity
(Dr. Kingsley Fletcher)

PART I

WHY MOST BELIEVERS NO LONGER PRACTICE PRAYER AND FASTING

INTRODUCTION
TO PART I

For many people, cultures, and traditions, January 1 is a day of feasting—a day for pork and sauerkraut, partying and singing.

For the members of Life Community Church, January 1 means it's time to start fasting. We ring in every new year by calling a solemn fast upon the church and by encouraging an atmosphere of prayer and fasting throughout our congregation.

We look forward to this time and eagerly await it throughout the year because we know that prayer and fasting results in spiritual feasting. We believe God for supernatural things, and we are blessed to see them. *"A cord of three strands is not quickly broken"* (Ecclesiastes 4:12), and we see the truth of this verse every year as we intertwine our prayers through a season of fasting. This practice brings unity to the body of Christ and establishes Jesus' lordship here on earth.

Unfortunately many in the faith community have yet to experience the power of prayer and fasting. A lot of believers have abandoned prayer and fasting altogether, while others have never even tried it. God is saddened by this because He makes us powerful in the Spirit through prayer and fasting. At the same time, Satan is

19

delighted when we abandon prayer and fasting because without the power of the Spirit, we can never stand against the enemy.

> MANY HAVE YET
> TO EXPERIENCE
> THE POWER
> OF PRAYER
> AND FASTING.

Why have believers fallen out of the habit of prayer and fasting? Why have many believers never even developed this habit? To bring lasting reform, we must understand the answers to these questions. We can only overcome the many barriers to prayer and fasting by recognizing—and avoiding—those barriers.

It is time for the church to call on God and do what God has called it to do—and that is pray and fast.

ONE

The Lack of Results in the Past

ISAIAH 58:1–12

Shout it aloud, do not hold back. Raise your voice like a trumpet. Declare to my people their rebellion and to the house of Jacob their sins. For day after day they seek me out; they seem eager to know my ways, as if they were a nation that does what is right and has not forsaken the commands of its God. They ask me for just decisions and seem eager for God to come near them. "Why have we fasted," they say, "and you have not seen it? Why have we humbled ourselves, and you have not noticed?" Yet on the day of your fasting, you do as you please and exploit all your workers. Your fasting ends in quarreling and strife, and in striking each other with wicked fists. You cannot fast as you do today and expect your voice to be heard on high. Is this the kind of fast I have chosen, only a day for a man to humble himself? Is it only for bowing one's head like a reed and for lying on sackcloth and ashes? Is that what you call a fast, a day acceptable to the LORD? Is not this the kind of fasting I have chosen: to loose the chains of injustice and untie the cords of the yoke, to set the oppressed free and break every yoke? Is it not to share your food with the hungry and to provide the poor wanderer with shelter—when you see the naked, to clothe him, and not to turn away from your own flesh and blood? Then your light will break forth like the dawn, and your healing will quickly appear; then your righteousness will go before you, and the glory of the LORD will be your rear guard. Then you will call, and the LORD will answer; you will cry for help, and he will say: Here am I. If you do away with the yoke of oppression, with the pointing finger and malicious talk, and if you spend yourselves in behalf of the hungry and satisfy the needs of the oppressed, then your light will rise in the darkness, and your night will become like the noonday. The LORD will guide you always; he will satisfy your needs in a sun-scorched land and will strengthen your frame. You will be like a well-watered garden, like a spring whose waters never fail. Your people will rebuild the ancient ruins and will raise up the age-old foundations; you will be called Repairer of Broken Walls, Restorer of Streets with Dwellings.

THE LACK OF RESULTS IN THE PAST

I magine how unwise it would be for a student to stop studying because he failed the last test for which he studied. Is this logical? Should he never study again for fear of another bad grade? Of course not! He might need to study *differently*, but no matter what, he still needs to study. The problem was with the way he studied—not with the act of studying itself.

Unfortunately some people abandon prayer and fasting for similar reasons: because they don't seem to be getting the desired results. But can the problem lie with God? Can we blame prayer and fasting, which He has ordained, for the lack of results? Or is it our own approach and our own attitudes that are at fault?

When you pray and fast and do not experience a breakthrough, there may be something in *your* life that needs to be addressed. God doesn't need to change; you do.

FASTING: THEN AND NOW

The people of Isaiah's time fasted without result. They were offended by God's apparent silence and asked Him for an explanation. Why was He not answering His people and honoring their sacrifices?

In many ways, the church today can be compared to the people of Isaiah's time. We, too, seek after God's leading, wanting to know His will for our lives.

For day after day they seek me out; they seem eager to know my ways. (Isaiah 58:2)

Many nations were supposedly founded upon godly principles, and despite the infiltration of immorality and debauchery into the very heart of our modern culture, a majority of people are still very religious—or at least think they are.

As if they were a nation that does what is right and has not forsaken the commands of its God. (verse 2)

As people of faith, we are also very concerned with social justice. We are against abortion, pornography, euthanasia, and the spread of illegal drugs, and we want to demonstrate our feelings on these important subjects. We want to see positive changes in our society, just as the people of Isaiah's day did:

They ask me for just decisions. (verse 2)

Just like these men and women of Isaiah's day, we *"seem eager for God to come near"* and we *"delight in approaching to God"* (verse 2 KJV). It seems that we, like Israel, have a lot going for us, a lot to commend. But unfortunately, like Israel, our fasting often produces no visible results, and it seems as if God does not hear our prayers.

"Why have we fasted," they say, "and you have not seen it? Why have we humbled ourselves, and you have not noticed?" (verse 3)

THE LACK OF RESULTS IN THE PAST
THE REST OF THE PROBLEM

"Why have we humbled ourselves, and you have not noticed?" This sounds like a good question to me. These people thought they were serving God wholeheartedly. They believed His Word, continued their religious traditions, and worked for social justice in their day. Yet nothing was happening. Results were nowhere to be seen.

Why?

The answer God gave them may surprise some believers:

Yet on the day of your fasting, you do as you please and exploit all your workers. Your fasting ends in quarreling and strife, and in striking each other with wicked fists. You cannot fast as you do today and expect your voice to be heard on high. Is this the kind of fast I have chosen...?   (verses 3–5)

The problem was that these people "did as they pleased." If the people of Isaiah's day were getting nowhere spiritually because they were pleasure seekers, then we are really in trouble in the opening years of the twenty-first century. A great percentage of our time, effort, and money are now spent on things that bring us pleasure—and the jobs that make pleasure seeking financially doable.

For many of us, nothing is more important than our jobs—*nothing*. Pleasure seeking and jobs are the two reasons most believers don't fast. We have many "more important" things to do, and fasting simply does not fit into the schedule. There is no time for it. This attitude prevents many from seeing answers to their prayers.

> IF GOD IS NOT ANSWERING OUR PRAYERS, SOMETHING IS WRONG—WITH US.

If God is not answering our prayers, something is wrong—with us, not with God. Our attitude may be wrong. Our concept of God may be wrong. Our behavior may be wrong. If we really put God first, we will see His blessings. But if we put Him second or third or fourth, results may be hard to see. To put it another way, if having fun is more important to us than having God's favor on our lives, there is not much hope for our spiritual future. If our jobs are more important to us than doing the will of God, then we are in serious trouble.

WHEN MOTIVES ARE WRONG

In Isaiah's day, those who fasted actually had an evil purpose in doing so.

> *Behold, ye fast for strife and debate, and to smite with the fist of wickedness: ye shall not fast as ye do this day, to make your voice to be heard on high. Is it such a fast that I have chosen?*
>
> (verses 4–5 KJV)

God went on to declare that this was *not* the fast He had chosen.

> *Is it only for bowing one's head like a reed and for lying on sackcloth and ashes? Is that what you call a fast, a day acceptable to the LORD?*   (verse 5)

We must guard our motives when fasting. If our intent is evil, the results won't be good.

Another thing to watch out for is a boastful attitude. When we fast, it's easy to fall into the sin of self-righteousness. The Pharisees made much of their fasting by putting on sackcloth and ashes, for instance, and the result was a big show of their piety. Prayer and fasting is not for the purpose of showing off. It is a very personal act performed unto God, not unto men. The fast that pleases God is anything but showy.

> *Is not this the kind of fasting I have chosen: to loose the chains of injustice and untie the cords of the yoke, to set the oppressed free and break every yoke? Is it not to share your food with the hungry and to provide the poor wanderer with shelter—when you see the naked, to clothe him, and not to turn away from your own flesh and blood?* (verses 6–7)

Our purpose for fasting is to *"loose the chains of injustice,"* to *"untie the cords of the yoke,"* to *"set the oppressed free,"* and to *"break every yoke."* These are the things that touch the heart of God. When we begin praying the heart of God and fasting for the desires of His heart, we will see results. Our motives are very wrong if we *only* fast for a new car, a new house, or even a spouse. We will be disappointed with the result.

BIBLICAL PRAYER AND FASTING ALWAYS BRINGS THE DESIRED RESULT.

If you have been fasting and praying but not receiving answers, carefully check your attitude. Open your heart, and God will show you where you have erred. If you have been discouraged to pray and fast because of a lack of results in the past, God is giving you another chance. Return to biblical prayer and fasting—which always brings the desired result.

Two

The Recent Emphasis on Faith as a Cure-All

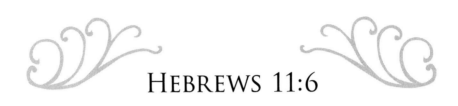

HEBREWS 11:6

And without faith it is impossible to please God,
because anyone who comes to him must believe
that he exists and that he rewards those
who earnestly seek him.

THE RECENT EMPHASIS ON FAITH AS A CURE-ALL

T raditionally, prayer and fasting has been one of the strong points of evangelical, Pentecostal, and charismatic doctrine. Yet today, even those groups have stopped fasting. Why do so few modern-day believers fast? Why have a majority of the evangelicals and Pentecostals stopped fasting?

For some of our Spirit-filled brothers and sisters, it was the discovery of the "Word of faith" and its operation that led to the abandonment of prayer and fasting. "Just speak the Word," many said, "and anything is possible." When believers discovered that, by simply exercising the promises of God, they could move heaven, they decided prayer and fasting were no longer necessary. Nothing could be further from the truth! It is sensitivity to the Spirit of God that gives us power to exercise the Word of God properly. And this sensitivity to His Spirit comes through prayer and fasting.

HOW FASTING FITS WITH FAITH

Some have turned to prophecy as a substitute for miracles, but prophecy was not meant to be a substitute for miracles. Prophecy is wonderful, and the Bible tells us not to despise prophecy (1 Thessalonians 5:20). But prophecy without the supernatural is not biblical prophecy at all. We need demonstration of the power of God in our lives.

To maintain crowds in their ministries when the miracles are gone, many people turn to gimmicks. Slowly, they begin to trust more and more in the world, instead of the Word, for their guidance. Many don't even realize what is happening to them—until it is too late.

SENSITIVITY TO THE SPIRIT COMES THROUGH PRAYER AND FASTING.

Emphasis on faith and the need to exercise it is not a bad thing. The Bible is clear: *"Without faith it is impossible to please God"* (Hebrews 11:6). Faith pleases God, but faith cannot bring you everything that you need. The key phrase here is *"those who earnestly seek him"* (verse 6). Faith depends upon a strong relationship with God. A strong relationship with God can be built by seeking Him. And prayer and fasting is the best way to do that.

Those who emphasize super-faith say that when things don't go well for you, it is because you don't have enough faith. But this leads to all kinds of wrong conclusions. If all you need is more faith, for instance, then why pray? Prayer is hard work. Why do it if it is not necessary? If all we need is faith, then why fast? Fasting is not enjoyable to the flesh. Why do it if we don't have to? If we are saved and on our way to heaven, then why not just enjoy this Christian life? Why not just settle in what we believe?

That all sounds good, but what we are not told is that in order to maintain a strong faith, and in order and to be effective in the kingdom of God, we must maintain a strong relationship with our heavenly Father. This is done through prayer and fasting.

The Recent Emphasis on Faith as a Cure-All

"O unbelieving and perverse generation," Jesus replied, "how long shall I stay with you? How long shall I put up with you? Bring the boy here to me." (Matthew 17:17)

When Jesus' disciples brought to Him a child whom they were unable to help, He called them an *"unbelieving and perverse generation"* and asked them, *"How long shall I stay with you? How long shall I put up with you?"* How could Jesus say that to His disciples? These men had left everything to follow Him. They had made great sacrifices to be at His side.

What He did next helps to explain His words. He called for the child. Then He *"rebuked the demon."* The result was that *"it came out of the boy, and he was healed from that moment"* (verse 18). It was so easy for Jesus. Just a word from Him was sufficient. He had power and authority. No demon could stand against Him. When He spoke, demons obeyed. He expected His disciples to have this same power. When they didn't, He chastened them.

Is it easy for us to deliver epileptics today? It can be—if we are prepared. But most of us are not. We struggle with the situations of life: problems in the workplace, tensions at home, difficulties in the church, and most of all, battles we face with our own characters. We quote promises and exercise faith, but nothing seems to change. Jesus wanted to show us that it can be easy—if we are prepared, as He was prepared.

No wonder that many who profess faith are weak! No wonder we are not expecting miracles! Most people have stopped seeking God in prayer and fasting.

If you have faith like a mustard seed, Jesus said, you can speak to mountains, telling them to move, and they will obey you. Faith makes the impossible possible. It brings into the realm of reality what can otherwise only be dreamed of. Faith goes beyond what the natural eye sees. According to Hebrews, *"Faith is the substance of things hoped for, the evidence of things not seen"* (Hebrews 11:1 KJV).

God can be perceived only by faith. His creation of the world and everything that is in it can be understood only by faith. His Word can be accepted only by faith. And Jesus said that if we have just a little faith, we can move mountains. Faith changes everything. Faith makes everything possible. Faith unlocks every door and opens every opportunity to the believer.

> SOME THINGS WILL NEVER COME TO PASS WITHOUT PRAYER AND FASTING.

Without prayer and fasting, however, our faith cannot function. Some miracles will never happen without prayer and fasting. Some circumstances will never change without prayer and fasting. Some situations will never be reversed without prayer and fasting. Prayer and fasting sharpen your expectancy so that, when you ask, you expect to receive.

THE NEED FOR BALANCE

The promises of God are conditional upon our living the life He has outlined for us. For instance, God delights to feed His children. David said,

> *I was young and now I am old, yet I have never seen the righteous forsaken or their children begging bread.* (Psalms 37:25)

This doesn't mean that we can do nothing and still receive everything, which many have been teaching. "Just speak the word in faith," we have heard over and over. That is not a wrong teaching, but it is not a complete teaching. Many people have exercised their faith for big cars, big houses, and big bank accounts, yet their souls are leaner today than they were ten years ago. They get fewer answers to prayer now than before. They may be living large, but they don't have the power of God in their lives.

If you are one of those who is eager to overcome error and to know truth, and if you have been concerned about the deceptive teaching that faith is a cure-all, please keep reading. God wants to teach you the balanced Word. He wants to make your faith effective. He wants to lead you into a life of communion with Him that will bring you the victories you have so desired. And this can only happen when you bolster your faith through prayer and fasting.

THREE

The Prevalence of the Spirit of Gluttony

PHILIPPIANS 3:17–19 KJV

Brethren, be followers together of me, and mark them
which walk so as ye have us for an ensample. (For many walk,
of whom I have told you often, and now tell you even weeping,
that they are the enemies of the cross of Christ: whose
end is destruction, whose God is their belly, and whose
glory is in their shame, who mind earthly things.)

THE PREVALENCE OF THE SPIRIT OF GLUTTONY

There is an idol in the land vying for attention. His name is *food*. He was already at work in Paul's day, and he's still at work today. He is also known as the belly god. Food is one of the most powerful gods at work in our society. In many places, he rules supreme.

HE'S CREPT INTO THE LIVES OF BELIEVERS...

The sad thing is that food rules many believers. Many of us work not to the glory of God or for the good of His kingdom but for daily bread. If Jesus Himself were to appear to us in the flesh and call us to forsake all—our homes, our jobs, everything—and follow Him, most of us would consider it to be a trick of the devil and would avoid obeying at all costs. Very little is more important to us than our jobs, because they produce food.

The best-attended activities these days are banquets, breakfasts, picnics, and barbecues. When we call for those who will travail for the purpose of God to be revealed or for revival for a city or a nation, we can count on one hand those who show up. In order to assure people's attendance at church activities, many times we have to promise a potluck, a Mexican feast, a special Italian dinner, or some kind of food.

Most well-attended conventions across the country advertise their good food. How many people would attend these activities if no food was served? How many would show up for several days of prayer and fasting? Food has become our idol.

WHOM WILL YOU SERVE THIS DAY?

At the same time that we are worshipping at the altar of food, we are saying to God, "God, we want to see Your power and glory."

God is saying to us, "You are not really serious. You don't mean what you are saying. You are just playing with words."

Do we really want to see God's power and glory? Do we really want a new anointing upon our lives? Do we really want to see a spiritual breakthrough in our nations, in our governments, in our homes, in our marriages, in the lives of our children, and in our own personal experiences with God?

FOOD IS ONE OF THE MOST POWERFUL GODS AT WORK IN OUR SOCIETY.

Why is it that we have quoted the Word from Genesis to Revelation and yet nothing is happening? Have we tried prayer and fasting? Perhaps our god, food, has not permitted us to do that.

Food is so important to us today. When men consider marriage, often they look for a woman who is a good cook, not a woman who loves God. To these men, an ideal woman is one who will faithfully have a delicious meal ready for them when they get home from work.

THE PREVALENCE OF THE SPIRIT OF GLUTTONY

This is a far more serious matter than we might think. The apostle Paul called such people *"enemies of the cross of Christ"* (Philippians 3:18 KJV). He knew that there were more important things to life. He was determined to *"press toward the mark for the prize of the high calling of God in Christ Jesus"* (verse 14 KJV). Concerning those whose god was Belly, those who were more concerned with *"earthly things"* (verse 19 KJV) than with the will of God for their lives, Paul predicted that their end would be *"destruction"* (verse 19 KJV).

Any time God's people cease to embrace the godly practice of prayer and fasting, they begin an inexorable slide toward *"destruction."* Any time believers give in to the god food, their glory becomes *"shame"* (verse 19 KJV). Any time we are more concerned about *"earthly things"* than about spiritual things, we are headed for ruin. People of faith cannot prevail under such circumstances. This is not my word. This is the eternal Word of God. Giving in to our appetites, or self-indulgence, is sin, and it separates us from the presence and blessing of God.

> SELF-INDULGENCE SEPARATES US FROM THE PRESENCE AND BLESSING OF GOD.

When God delivered His people from bondage in Egypt and sent them on their way to the Promised Land, occasionally they were tempted to go back, despite what they had suffered in Egypt. What could make people want to return to slavery? You guessed it: food.

> *We remember the fish we ate in Egypt at no cost—also the cucumbers, melons, leeks, onions and garlic.*   (Numbers 11:5)

While some were remembering the amazing way in which God sent the plagues upon Egypt and the way He destroyed the Egyptian army in the Red Sea, others were thinking of what they had grown accustomed to eating around the fires in Goshen. They were not rejoicing about manna from heaven; they were longing for leeks and cucumbers in slavery.

That may surprise some people, but it doesn't surprise me. I know believers who can remember exactly what they had to eat at a special gathering twenty years ago and who prepared it, yet they cannot remember who was saved in the last revival or when they last had a burden to pray for people in need.

Many people actually live by their stomachs. It is their clock. When they get hungry in the morning, they know it is time to get up. When they feel hungry later in the day, they know it is lunchtime. When they get hungry again, they get excited because they know it is quitting time. These people even dream about food. Are these people really believers? Well, they call themselves believers, but they are unaware of the fact that a strange idol has taken control of their lives.

A HIGHER CALL

God has not ordained that we be ruled by our appetites. The Christian life means freedom from our appetites. When we are slaves to our appetites, we are carnally minded. And the carnal, or sinful, mind is God's enemy.

> *The sinful mind is hostile to God. It does not submit to God's law, nor can it do so.* (Romans 8:7)

Being a believer and being dominated by appetite are two incompatible things. The two are so contrary to each other that they cannot coexist. They simply do not go together.

Many have fallen into this deceit because of the popular belief that we simply must give special attention to food in order to exist. I am glad that Jesus addressed that belief and cleared things up for all eternity when He said, *"Man shall not live by bread alone, but by* every word that proceedeth out of the mouth of God" (Matthew 4:4 KJV).

Jesus taught us to labor for lasting values, for that which does not perish:

> Do not work for food that spoils, but for food that endures to eternal life, which the Son of Man will give you. On him God the Father has placed his seal of approval. (John 6:27)

BEING A BELIEVER AND BEING DOMINATED BY APPETITE ARE NOT COMPATIBLE.

Food is not a very good god. It perishes. When we eat it, we feel satisfied for a very short time. How much better it is to put our efforts into lasting things! And how sad it is to lose the blessing of God for something so insignificant and temporal as food!

WHEN GLUTTONY TAKES OVER

Food has become so important to some of us that we let it have preeminence in our lives. If you are consumed by gluttony, hear the Word of the Lord:

> When you sit to dine with a ruler, note well what is before you, and put a knife to your throat if you are given to gluttony. Do not crave his delicacies, for that food is deceptive. Do not wear yourself out to get rich; have the wisdom to show restraint. (Proverbs 23:1–4)

"Put a knife to your throat" in this verse does not mean "commit suicide." It means to suppress your appetites. Gluttony leads to other sins, and if you don't get control over it, it will control you.

"Have the wisdom to show restraint." You think you know how to handle life, but God knows so much better than you. He is telling you to get control over your natural appetites before they get control over you, because, once again, gluttony *will* control you.

Gluttony can even lead to poverty.

For drunkards and gluttons become poor, and drowsiness clothes them in rags.   (Proverbs 23:21)

According to the Bible, *"gluttons"* are in the same class with *"drunkards."* Both of them will *"become poor."* Yet to believers, the most popular occasions are Thanksgiving, Christmas, the annual picnic, and New Year's Eve—all occasions for special feasting.

> GET CONTROL OVER YOUR APPETITES BEFORE THEY GET CONTROL OVER YOU.

What does Thanksgiving mean to the average citizen today? It means food! Because of that, many people in America have stopped calling the day "Thanksgiving" and started calling it "Turkey Day."

What does Christmas mean for a lot of people? Christmas cookies, cheese logs, fruitcakes, and baked ham.

What does Easter mean for many? Candy eggs, jelly beans, chocolate bunnies, and another baked ham.

No wonder we have lost the power of God! No wonder poverty has overtaken the church! No wonder the kingdom of darkness is advancing on every front!

Our families are in crisis. Our nations are in crisis. We are crying out, "Oh God, raise up men and women who can touch You in prayer and bring revival to our nation," but we finish the prayer quickly because everyone is hungry and wants to eat before the food gets cold. Is it any wonder that our prayers are not prevailing?

KEEPING OUR APPETITES IN CHECK

James said of Elijah,

Elijah was a man just like us. He prayed earnestly that it would not rain, and it did not rain on the land for three and a half years. Again he prayed, and the heavens gave rain, and the earth produced its crops. (James 5:17–18)

James was careful not to give us the impression that Elijah was some superhuman. He was *"a man just like us."* He was just as human as any one of us, yet his prayers prevailed. When he asked God to close the heavens, the heavens were closed. When he asked God for rain, it rained.

Did God just choose Elijah and sovereignly decide to favor him above others? I don't believe so. I believe that Elijah had power with God because he fasted and prayed, got control of his appetites, and developed a strong relationship with his heavenly Father.

It is true that God wants to feed His children, but He never intended for food to dominate our lives. God gave us sex, but He intended sex to be kept within the confines of the marriage. God gave us plants, but He never intended for us to smoke them and inject their ingredients into our veins for false "highs." Everything has its purpose. We were not destined to be controlled by food.

To many people, the most important thing to do on payday is go to the grocery store. They wouldn't miss it for anything. Some people are slaves to Popcorn. Some serve the god Sausage. Some are bound by Chocolate. When these people hear the word *fast*, they are frightened. They think they might die if they fast.

Food, for many, is like a security blanket. It comforts them and causes them not to be afraid. They have developed a dependency on it.

Those who go through periods of depression sometimes go to the refrigerator often, every ten minutes or so, looking for something to soothe their frayed nerves. People who can't sleep at night sneak down to the refrigerator, hoping to find something there that will help them to rest. For some, their dependency on food is just as serious as an alcohol or drug dependency. They have been tricked by the enemy of their souls into making food an idol, and Satan is delighted!

To these people, doing without food for even one day seems like a most horrible prospect. They cannot conceive of life without their idol. Taking food away from them means taking away the joy of life. They look forward to mealtimes. What else is there to live for?

FOOD, FOR MANY, IS LIKE A SECURITY BLANKET; THEY ARE DEPENDENT ON IT.

Many people know that they should fast, and they want to fast, but they can't. They don't know how to break the food habit. They don't know how to get their thoughts and their emotions under control long enough to seek God seriously. Satan is having a field day diverting the attention of God's people away from Him.

When you turn on the television today, you see what broadcasters have determined viewers want to see: scandals, sex, violence, and food. (A cooking segment has recently become a regular evening news feature of a major Washington, D.C., station because that is what the people want.)

Many people are actually drunk on food. They are under the influence of what they eat, and they need deliverance. As believers, we take pride in the fact that we are not enslaved to the things that used to bind us. We are no longer captive to gambling or addicted to drugs and alcohol. Yet many of us are even more addicted to food now than we were before we became believers, and we live for our stomachs instead of for our Lord!

When I first came to America many years ago, I was shocked by what I witnessed. Everywhere I went, people were offering me food. It is impolite to refuse an offer of hospitality, so I ate what was set before me and drank enough Kool-Aid to sink a battleship.

Pastors are not without blame in all of this. Sometimes pastors are the worst offenders. It almost seems as though some rush through their sermons so they can get home and have Sunday dinner.

If a pastor is a glutton, how can he care for the spiritual needs of the flock over which God has placed him? How can he help his members to be delivered from their bad habits? How can he give spiritual direction to others when he has an idol in his own life?

Pastors, if banquets are more important to us than prayer and fasting, we are in trouble. Let us arise and declare that the principal reason many believers do not get answers to prayer is that they never fast. Let us declare that because food has become a god in our society, abstaining from food is one of the surest ways to find God's perfect will for our lives. Let us be bold to make known that, in these difficult days, we simply will not make it without lives dedicated to prayer and fasting.

FOUR

The Selfish Spirit
of the Age

PROVERBS 16:26 KJV

He that laboureth
laboureth for himself;
for his mouth craveth it of him.

THE SELFISH SPIRIT
OF THE AGE

The mind-set in today's society is one of complete self-ishness. Our economy trains us to look after our own interests. Our children are trying to be independent and self-sufficient earlier and earlier. Even as believers, we stick to ourselves and look out for number one. Instead of showing concern for our neighbors, as Jesus taught, the theme today is total self-reliance.

This is one of the major reasons many believers have stopped fasting. They are getting along just fine without it. They can pay the bills and still have a little left over. There's nothing to worry about, so why fast? If and when some tragedy does strike, they are unprepared—but by then, it is usually too late to fast.

SELFISH FASTING

Not everyone has abandoned fasting. But what are we fasting for? Are we fasting for a promotion at work or favor with the boss? Or are we fasting for the needs of others rather than just our own?

WHEN KINGS PRAY AND FAST

Who has a burden to fast for the nation? Who has a burden to fast for its leaders? Who has a burden to fast for the community? Who has a burden to fast for drug addicts? Who has a burden to fast for those who are sick and afflicted?

Many congregations today are only concerned with excellence in attendance, in program, and in reputation. The questions that consume them are:

- Do we have the largest building?
- Do we have the best attendance on Sunday morning?
- Do we have the most money?

When we are caught up in such petty concerns, the devil doesn't have anything to worry about. His kingdom will never be endangered by such a limited vision.

> GOD IS ASKING US, "WHY CAN'T I GET ANYTHING FROM YOU?"

As individuals, we are selfish in our worship. Many times we go to God in worship only to present our wish lists. Even those who experience the anointing of God's Spirit want to use that anointing for themselves and their desires. When they pray, they keep asking, "Why can't I get anything from God? Why can't I get anything from God?" At the same time, God is asking them, "Why can't I get anything from *you*? Why can't I get anything from *you*?"

God wants us to *"undo the heavy burdens"* (Isaiah 58:6 KJV). He wants us to *"let the oppressed go free"* (verse 6 KJV). If we could just forget ourselves for a few minutes and seek the mind of the Lord, we would see the greatness He has prepared for us. If we could get to know what is in the heart of the Father, prayer and fasting would take on a whole new meaning for us.

THE PROBLEM WITH MONEY

Believers who visit a third-world country usually come back impressed by several things: the poverty-stricken state of that nation, the sincerity of the people of that nation, and the intense commitment of believers in that nation to the Lord, His church, and His people.

Unfortunately, those of us in more developed nations usually don't evidence that same intense commitment to the Lord. If Jesus appeared today in the flesh and called us to serve Him, the first thing many would ask Him would be, "What's the pay and how are the benefits?" That is how selfish we have become!

If our interest in earning money was for the purpose of using that money to further the kingdom of God, that would be one thing. Most believers, however, are interested in money solely for the pleasures and comforts it brings. Many believers are even robbing God of the tithes due to Him so that they can enjoy more of the "good life." When they were poor, they faithfully tithed; but now that God has prospered them, they never have enough. They take the tithe and use it for more luxuries. They think God owes them a good time in life, and they think everything should be used for their pleasure. They swallow up the enemy's enticing argument, "You worked hard; now enjoy it."

The problem is that when we are selfishly oriented, there never seems to be enough. Consider the parable that Jesus told about a young man who was prospering:

The ground of a certain rich man produced a good crop. He thought to himself, "What shall I do? I have no place to store my crops." Then he said, "This is what I'll do. I will tear down my barns and build bigger ones, and there I will store all my grain and my goods. And I'll say to myself, 'You have plenty of good things laid up for many years. Take life easy; eat, drink and be merry.'" But God said to him, "You fool! This very night your life will be demanded from you. Then who will get what you have prepared for yourself?" This is how it will be with anyone who stores up things for himself but is not rich toward God.

(Luke 12:16–21)

This man fell for Satan's line. He had worked hard and was rich beyond his wildest dreams. What would he do with his newfound wealth? He decided to flaunt his good fortune and lavish the wealth upon himself. And for this, he paid dearly. Because he laid up treasure for himself and was not rich toward God, his end was sad. That very night his life was required of him. Isn't it ironic that selfishness robs us of the very blessings we seek?

There are two important lessons for us to learn from this parable. The first is that riches never satisfy. The book of Ecclesiastes, written by the wisest man ever, records this point again and again:

To the man who pleases him, God gives wisdom, knowledge and happiness, but to the sinner he gives the task of gathering and storing up wealth to hand it over to the one who pleases God. This too is meaningless, a chasing after the wind.

(Ecclesiastes 2:26, emphasis added)

There was a man all alone; he had neither son nor brother. There was no end to his toil, yet his eyes were not content with his wealth. "For whom am I toiling," he asked, "and why am I depriving myself of enjoyment?" This too is meaningless—a miserable business!

(Ecclesiastes 4:8, emphasis added)

Whoever loves money never has money enough; whoever loves wealth is never satisfied with his income. This too is meaningless.

(Ecclesiastes 5:10, emphasis added)

The Selfish Spirit of the Age

*All man's efforts are for his mouth, yet **his appetite is never satisfied**.* (Ecclesiastes 6:7, emphasis added)

The second lesson we must learn from Jesus' parable is that when God prospers us with material things, it is not so that we can turn away from Him and give ourselves to those things. When He prospers us, it is not so that we can spend more time with our possessions and neglect time with Him. When He prospers us, it is not so that we can develop uncontrollable appetites that prevent us from seeking the God who formed us. God prospers us so that the vision for His kingdom can be established, so that we can be a blessing to others.

> WHEN GOD PROSPERS US, IT IS SO WE CAN BE BLESSINGS TO OTHERS.

A Richer Kind of Rich

Right up until the day of the flood, the people in Noah's day were busy *"eating and drinking"* (Matthew 24:38). In many people's minds, this is what prosperity is all about: plenty of food and plenty of drink.

The prosperity that God gives, however, is much deeper and much richer!

That presumptuous rich farmer in Luke 12 had a lot to learn.

And I'll say to myself, "You have plenty of good things laid up for many years. Take life easy; eat, drink and be merry."
(Luke 12:19)

How smug! He thought he had life all figured out. He thought he knew it all. What a great surprise he had coming!

WHEN KINGS PRAY AND FAST

Selfish people never pray and fast. Prayer and fasting take time, time that can't be spent on something else. Prayer and fasting take effort, effort that you can't put toward some other pursuit. That's what turns most believers off of prayer and fasting—all the time and effort involved. But the truth is, the investment in time and effort required for prayer and fasting is small compared to the spiritual riches that result.

When problems and critical decisions face a congregation, the members of that congregation need to join together in a period of prayer and fasting. Yet frequently you can count on many people being "too busy" to do their part. They have other "more important" things to do. When they have a need that touches them personally, though, they want everyone to join with them in prayer. Have all our prayers become selfish in nature? Is it all "me," "my," "mine," and "myself"?

No wonder God doesn't answer! We are way off base when we pray this way. Our attitudes are wrong. Our priorities are wrong. Our motivations are wrong. Our timing is wrong. To experience the riches of God, we need to get rid of this selfishness, humble ourselves, and willingly embark on periods of prayer and fasting.

REMOVE THE ROADBLOCKS

Getting rid of the selfishness in our lives is not an easy thing; it doesn't happen overnight. It takes time, patience, and the Holy Spirit's working in our lives. But that's not to say there's nothing we can do.

Take television, for example. Television advertising makes you selfish. It makes you want many things that will not help you at all and many other things that actually will be detrimental to your physical and spiritual well-being.

THE SELFISH SPIRIT OF THE AGE

Television not only makes you selfish; it makes your children selfish too. They want the things they see on television—whether they are good for them or not. Even worse, your children are making role models out of those they see on television. They are no longer imitating Mom and Dad. The posters hanging in their bedrooms let you know where their hearts are.

You may make excuses for them, such as, "This is just a passing fad." But the truth is that Satan has an intense campaign to win the souls of your children, to make them totally selfish. We must guard what our children see to prevent this from happening.

IF YOU ARE TOTALLY SELFISH, YOUR CHILDREN WILL BE TOO.

God has blessed my wife and me with two beautiful girls, Anna-Kissel and Damaris Joy, and I thank God for them. I try to teach them to honor the presence of God and to respect the house of God, just as David did:

> *I rejoiced with those who said to me, "Let us go to the house of the LORD."* (Psalms 122:1)

If I want my daughters to respect and love God, I must first model for them that respect and love. If you are totally selfish and are living a life of selfishness, it is impossible to teach your children to be selfless. If your job, your car, and your house take precedence over God and His house, your children's values will be the same.

God is interested in your job, your car, and the house in which you live, but He is interested in far more than those things alone. Why is it that most believers spend so much time believing God for these things when there is so much more wealth—spiritual wealth—to be had?

Get your priorities sorted out. Don't take your cue from this selfish world system but from the eternal Word of God. When you do, you will find prayer and fasting to be high on your list of priorities.

FIVE

The Lack of Teaching on the Subject of Prayer and Fasting

HOSEA 4:6

My people are destroyed from lack of knowledge.

THE LACK OF TEACHING ON THE SUBJECT OF PRAYER AND FASTING

M any believers do not practice the custom of prayer and fasting simply because they have never been taught about it. This is especially true with new converts. Older believers know about prayer and fasting because it was more commonly taught and practiced years ago. Today, however, it is a neglected practice.

Fasting is denounced in some religious circles. They teach that it is a pagan practice and even consider it heresy.

Others teach that fasting was only for a former time. The leaders of these churches never fast—and they also never experience miracles.

If fasting were not important and biblical, Jesus never would have fasted. He is our example—and He practiced fasting.

Among important Bible subjects, fasting has to take its place near the top. There is just as much teaching about prayer and fasting in the Bible as there is about many of the more commonly taught doctrines.

Having lost sight of fasting's importance and the benefits it holds, few Bible teachers take time to lay the biblical foundations necessary to build lives that are dedicated to prayer and fasting. As a result, some people are still unaware that fasting is even in the Bible.

There is a more malignant reason that many spiritual leaders no longer teach prayer and fasting: It is not a very popular subject. It is not something the ear likes to hear, and it is therefore shunned as "too controversial." Some would rather teach what people *want* to hear than what they *need* to hear.

> PRAYER AND FASTING WORKS; IT HAS BEEN ORDAINED BY GOD.

Fasting, to some people, seems absurd and illogical. How could abstinence from food have so many benefits? It doesn't seem to make scientific sense. But doesn't most of God's Word seem absurd to the natural mind? Aren't God's ways strange to all of us?

As the heavens are higher than the earth, so are my ways higher than your ways and my thoughts than your thoughts.
(Isaiah 55:9)

I have two doctorates—one in theology and one in philosophy—as well as a background in electrical engineering. Some might think it strange that such a well-educated man devotes so much of his time to such a "primitive" practice as prayer and fasting.

But I know that prayer and fasting works; it has been ordained by God for a divine purpose. Whether others understand this or not, I personally am determined to do God's will. I am determined—for the sake of my soul, my family, and my ministry to the world—to live a life dedicated to prayer and fasting, and to teach others the benefits of doing the same.

PART II

WHY I STILL BELIEVE IN PRAYER AND FASTING

Six

The Biblical Basis for Prayer and Fasting

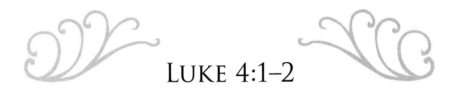

LUKE 4:1–2

Jesus, full of the Holy Spirit, returned from the Jordan and
was led by the Spirit in the desert, where for forty days
he was tempted by the devil. He ate nothing during
those days, and at the end of them he was hungry.

THE BIBLICAL BASIS FOR PRAYER AND FASTING

W
e saw in the last chapter that many do not practice prayer and fasting because there is a lack of teaching on the subject. This lack of teaching, however, is not for a lack of teaching materials. The practice of prayer and fasting is woven throughout the Scriptures; it is very clearly taught in the Bible.

BIBLICAL EXAMPLES

Moses, for instance, the servant whom God chose to lead Israel out of Egypt, practiced fasting. When he ascended Mt. Sinai to get the Law from the Lord, he fasted there in the Lord's presence on top of the mountain:

> *Moses was there with the LORD forty days and forty nights without eating bread or drinking water. And he wrote on the tablets the words of the covenant—the Ten Commandments.*
>
> (Exodus 34:28)

When the great Old Testament prophet Elijah was *"afraid and ran for his life"* (1 Kings 19:3), the Lord nourished him with sleep and a good meal, and then led him into a period of fasting:

Then he lay down under the tree and fell asleep. All at once an angel touched him and said, "Get up and eat." He looked around, and there by his head was a cake of bread baked over hot coals, and a jar of water. He ate and drank and then lay down again. The angel of the LORD came back a second time and touched him and said, "Get up and eat, for the journey is too much for you." So he got up and ate and drank. Strengthened by that food, he traveled forty days and forty nights until he reached Horeb, the mountain of God. (1 Kings 19:5–8)

These examples were from Old Testament times, but fasting continued in the New Testament as well. The prophetess Anna, who had the privilege of seeing the Messiah shortly after he was born, regularly practiced fasting:

There was also a prophetess, Anna, the daughter of Phanuel, of the tribe of Asher. She was very old; she had lived with her husband seven years after her marriage, and then was a widow until she was eighty-four. She never left the temple but worshiped night and day, fasting and praying. Coming up to them at that very moment, she gave thanks to God and spoke about the child to all who were looking forward to the redemption of Jerusalem. (Luke 2:36–38)

Paul, one of the greatest New Testament leaders, was ushered into his ministry through a time of fasting.

As he neared Damascus on his journey, suddenly a light from heaven flashed around him. He fell to the ground and heard a voice say to him, "Saul, Saul, why do you persecute me?" "Who are you, Lord?" Saul asked. "I am Jesus, whom you are persecuting," he replied. "Now get up and go into the city, and you will be told what you must do." The men traveling with Saul stood there speechless; they heard the sound but did not see anyone. Saul got up from the ground, but when he opened his eyes he

*could see nothing. So they led him by the hand into Damascus. For three days he was blind, and **did not eat or drink anything.***
(Acts 9:3–9, emphasis added)

At the end of those three days, God revealed to a disciple named Ananias that he should go and minister to Saul of Tarsus. After this, Saul, now Paul, received his healing and began a ministry that would take him all over the then-known world doing the works of God.

Since he wrote much of the New Testament, inspired by the Holy Spirit, a lot of our New Testament theology flowed from the pen of Paul. He also founded many of the early churches and taught their leaders. He believed strongly in the effectiveness of prayer and fasting, practiced it himself, and instructed others to do the same. Paul never forgot the lesson of prayer and fasting. In his second letter to the Corinthians, he told them that he had been *"in fastings often"* (2 Corinthians 11:27 KJV).

OUR GREATEST EXAMPLE, JESUS CHRIST, PRACTICED PRAYER AND FASTING.

Most important of all to us, Jesus, our greatest example, fasted.

And Jesus being full of the Holy Ghost returned from Jordan, and was led by the Spirit into the wilderness, being forty days tempted of the devil. And in those days he did eat nothing: and when they were ended, he afterward hungered.
(Luke 4:1–2 KJV)

Jesus was wise enough to know that, without the Father, He could do nothing. Because of this, He sought the Father through prayer and fasting. He waited in the Father's presence until He was endued with power from on high.

WHEN KINGS PRAY AND FAST

If this is how our Lord lived, how can we do any less? *"I tell you the truth, no servant is greater than his master, nor is a messenger greater than the one who sent him"* (John 13:16).

As a side note, many people believe that it is impossible to fast as Jesus did on this occasion. "Forty days is just too long!" they say. They think that anyone who tries to fast that long will die. But Jesus wasn't the only person in the Bible to fast forty days. As we saw earlier in this chapter, Moses and Elijah each fasted for forty days. Many people have done it successfully in modern times, as well. I have fasted forty days, and I didn't die from it. And you won't die either—if God tells you to go on an extended fast.

WHEN TO FAST

Not only does the Bible offer us many examples of people who practiced prayer and fasting, but it also shows us *when* to pray and fast. It gives us many examples of situations that require prayer and fasting. For example, like the prophet Daniel, we should fast during times of mourning:

> *In the third year of Cyrus king of Persia, a revelation was given to Daniel (who was called Belteshazzar). Its message was true and it concerned a great war. The understanding of the message came to him in a vision. At that time I, Daniel, mourned for three weeks. I ate no choice food; no meat or wine touched my lips; and I used no lotions at all until the three weeks were over.*
> (Daniel 10:1–3)

Ezra demonstrated this principle in the Old Testament, as well. He practiced prayer and fasting while mourning for the sins of Israel:

> *Ezra was praying and confessing, weeping and throwing himself down before the house of God....Then Ezra withdrew from*

before the house of God and went to the room of Jehohanan son of Eliashib. While he was there, he ate no food and drank no water, because he continued to mourn over the unfaithfulness of the exiles. (Ezra 10:1, 6)

According to the example found in Judges, we should fast during times of distress:

Then the Israelites drew near to Benjamin the second day. This time, when the Benjamites came out from Gibeah to oppose them, they cut down another eighteen thousand Israelites, all of them armed with swords. Then the Israelites, all the people, went up to Bethel, and there they sat weeping before the LORD. They fasted that day until evening and presented burnt offerings and fellowship offerings to the LORD. (Judges 20:24–26)

Prayer and fasting is also appropriate when we're seeking divine direction in spiritual matters or in everyday life decisions. The early church at Antioch, for instance, sought God's guidance regarding mission work; they obtained that guidance through prayer and fasting:

> WE SHOULD FAST DURING TIMES OF DISTRESS AND WHEN SEEKING GUIDANCE.

In the church at Antioch there were prophets and teachers: Barnabas, Simeon called Niger, Lucius of Cyrene, Manaen (who had been brought up with Herod the tetrarch) and Saul. While they were worshiping the Lord and fasting, the Holy Spirit said, "Set apart for me Barnabas and Saul for the work to which I have called them." (Acts 13:1–2)

In turn, Paul and Barnabas sought the Lord's direction in selecting spiritual leaders for the churches they ministered to.

[Paul and Barnabas] preached the good news in [Derbe] and won a large number of disciples. Then they returned to Lystra, Iconium and Antioch, strengthening the disciples and encouraging them to remain true to the faith. "We must go through many hardships to enter the kingdom of God," they said. Paul and Barnabas appointed elders for them in each church and, with prayer and fasting, committed them to the Lord, in whom they had put their trust. (Acts 14:21–23)

THE BIBLICAL SECRET TO PRAYER AND FASTING

If you want Bible results, you have to live the Bible way. The secret to success for each of these men and women in the Bible was that they were involved in the business of God's kingdom. When you get involved with kingdom business, sometimes you forget to eat. You have more important things—heavenly things—to think about. Your physical desires become much less important to you as you focus on your spiritual needs.

All the great religious reformers, as well as leaders throughout church history, carried on the biblical tradition of prayer and fasting. They learned the secret of seeking God and the importance of seeking God. We must continue this tradition, for it was established by the Lord Himself.

SEVEN

My Personal Experiences with Prayer and Fasting

JOHN 14:12–14

I tell you the truth, anyone who has faith in me will do what I have been doing. He will do even greater things than these, because I am going to the Father. And I will do whatever you ask in my name, so that the Son may bring glory to the Father. You may ask me for anything in my name, and I will do it.

My Personal Experiences with Prayer and Fasting

It's never changed; it's still the same today as it was when I was a teenager. When I was a young man, God would speak to me, and I would write everything down. He would wake me up and say, "Write, write, write, write." As I began to write, He would faithfully show me what to put down on paper.

When all this started, I was just a young man desiring to serve God and desiring to walk with Him. Because of this desire to walk with God, I would spend quality time alone with Him in prayer and fasting, seeking His face and searching out His will. I learned early on that when you seek Him, He will speak to you!

This is another reason why I believe in prayer and fasting: because I have seen its results in my life and in the lives of others. Why would I waste my time on God if He is dead? I wouldn't! And neither would you. If anyone asks you, you tell them that you serve a living God. And since He is alive, we have living experiences in the Christian life—not dead ones.

WHEN KINGS PRAY AND FAST
THREE GENERATIONS OF PRAYER AND FASTING

I have been blessed to see many of these "living experiences" throughout my life. From the time I was a child, I saw the mighty results that come from prayer and fasting as my parents were faithful to pray and fast unto the Lord. Their dedication to prayer and fasting influenced me, and now that same dedication is evident in my daughters' lives. Praise God for His faithfulness!

> *I, the LORD your God, am a jealous God, punishing the children for the sin of the fathers to the third and fourth generation of those who hate me, but **showing love to a thousand generations of those who love me and keep my commandments.***
> (Exodus 20:5–6, emphasis added)

THE FIRST GENERATION: MOM AND DAD

Some of my earliest memories are of my father taking a bottle of water and leaving the house so that he could find a solitary place to seek the face of God in extended prayer and fasting. He didn't go to a hotel. He preferred an unused stretch of beach where he could spend several days in God's presence. When he returned, I could see the anointing of God on his life.

My nephew had a serious health problem when he was young, something like epilepsy. I was there the day Daddy took him aside and laid hands on him. He said, "In the name of Jesus Christ, be healed." From that day on, he never suffered another attack. Today he is a preacher of the gospel.

God also gave me a praying mother. She has prayed for hours every day since I can remember. Prayer is her bread. Every night you can hear her praying, and I have never known her to spend a complete night in sleep. At three o'clock she is praying; at four o'clock she is praying; at five o'clock she is praying. She is always praying.

The dedication of my parents to lives of prayer and fasting kept me from going the way of the world. It saved my life on many occasions, and it put me on a straight course toward the ministry.

When I was only six, I was hospitalized with a serious eye injury. It was so severe that I was in a state of unconsciousness for three months and had to be fed intravenously. Three specialists—one from Africa and two from Europe—all gave up hope for my recovery. One of them told my mother, "I am very sorry. There is no hope for your son."

When my mother heard that dreaded verdict, she began walking all over the hospital, talking to God and interceding on my behalf. God told her that if she would enter into a period of serious prayer and fasting, He would spare my life. She obeyed God, and I miraculously recovered.

> MY PARENTS'
> DEDICATION TO
> FASTING SAVED
> MY LIFE ON MANY
> OCCASIONS.

THE SECOND GENERATION: ME

At the age of fifteen, I was one of seven teenagers who formed what we called "The Power House Evangelistic Ministries." Our goal was to go from village to village, city to city, and school to school, leading people to Christ.

Soon after we formed that group, I was led to enter into a three-day period of prayer and fasting for the first time. If God could use my parents, I thought, He could use me. I would seek His face until I heard from heaven and until His touch was upon my life.

WHEN KINGS PRAY AND FAST

During those days, I attended a meeting in the bush about three miles from my home. There I lay on my face before God and waited expectantly to know God's voice and to get clear directions. I desperately needed to know His perfect will for my life. I was afraid to move to the left or to the right without knowing His desire. (See Isaiah 30:21.) I told God that I would rather die than live without His blessing on my life.

Some people may think that such words, uttered by a fifteen-year-old, are not very important. But believe me—they are important to God. It is because of that prayer that I am where I am today.

> I TOLD GOD THAT I WOULD RATHER DIE THAN LIVE WITHOUT HIS BLESSING.

God revealed Himself to me during those days. One night in a service I had a glorious experience. As we were praying together in the church, I experienced what is known as a "trance." In old-fashioned Pentecostal terms, I "went out under the power of God." For the next three hours I was caught up in the Spirit. Other people were praying around me, but I was oblivious to what they were doing or saying.

My encounter with the Lord that night changed my life and my ministry. For the first time I saw the devil for who he really is. It was also during this encounter that I received an anointing to pray for the sick. From then on I had a new sense of urgency and a new sensitivity to the Spirit of God.

When I got up, someone asked me, "What happened? You were talking, but we couldn't understand what you were experiencing." I tried to explain to them, in the best way I could, what God had done in those three hours. I had been in the presence of God, and the experience forever changed the course of my life. Praise God for the prayer and fasting that ushered in that mighty, heavenly encounter!

The Third Generation: My Daughters

Because of God's goodness, prayer and fasting has impacted my daughters' lives, as well. When we went to Ghana in 1992, for example, my daughter fasted for three days. She didn't get out of bed one morning, and so I asked her, "Anna, won't you get up?"

She replied, "Daddy, I'm fasting."

For three days she didn't eat anything. She just fasted and prayed for the people of Ghana. She was only seven at the time, but she realized the importance of prayer and fasting. I was so proud of her—and still am—for being a minister of the gospel.

PRAYER AND FASTING
TEARS DOWN WALLS

Time and time again throughout my life, I have seen the powerful effects of dedicated prayer and fasting on believers' lives. I have witnessed yokes being destroyed, heavy burdens being undone, and the works of the enemy being brought to naught—all because someone fasted, prayed, and sought the face of God.

As I shared earlier, my parents were never afraid of Satan or his hordes of demons. They approached him under the anointing of the Holy Spirit, and because of this, they always had victory. He respected them. When they spoke to him to leave, he could only answer, "Yes sir! Yes ma'am!" He could not resist them but had to submit to their authority, because it was the Spirit's authority working through them.

No wonder Satan tries to keep us from fasting! No wonder he offers every conceivable excuse to the flesh! No wonder he lulls

God's people to sleep! He hates prayer and fasting because it releases God's anointing on our lives.

FASTING MIXED WITH FAITH

When foreign missionaries first came to our part of Africa, we didn't have any fancy meeting places. There were no buildings that would accommodate us, so we met in the bush to sing the praises of God. Occasionally we would gather and pray all night. During the night it would sometimes rain—except in the spot where we were gathered. God protected us.

> SATAN HATES PRAYER AND FASTING BECAUSE IT RELEASES GOD'S ANOINTING.

Many of our outdoor crusades were likewise threatened by rain. When this would happen, we just commanded the rain to wait until the meeting had ended—and it did. We had such simple faith in God, and He honored that faith.

Some years ago, when a group of Americans went with me to Africa for meetings, they saw a demonstration of this faith in action. Heavy rains came during our stay and threatened to disrupt our outdoor activities. The archbishop in charge, Benson Idahosa of Nigeria, boldly declared on national radio and television that the crusade would not be suspended and that rain would not interfere with what God wanted to do.

During the meeting cripples got up and walked; blind people were able to see for the very first time; and other outstanding miracles were performed in the name of the Lord. It was already raining in other parts of the city, but we were spared so that God could work in the lives of the great crowd of people who had gathered. When we had said the final "amen" of the crusade, it began pouring rain, and everyone had to scurry for cover. This is typical of the simple miracles that God does on the African continent in answer to the simple faith of the African believers.

God Works *Today*

The miracles that we saw in Africa were not the result of a well-developed theology. We had few textbooks. What God did was in response to our dedication to seeking His face and His will for our lives.

When we read His Word, we believed it—and He performed it. John 14:12–14 was one of our favorite passages from the Bible.

> *Verily, verily, I say unto you, He that believeth on me, the works that I do shall he do also; and greater works than these shall he do; because I go unto my Father. And whatsoever ye shall ask in my name, that will I do, that the Father may be glorified in the Son. If ye shall ask any thing in my name, I will do it.*
>
> (John 14:12–14 KJV)

John 14 is frequently used at funeral services to talk about our future glory. Most pastors, however, read only the first part of the chapter; they dwell on the future promises. "We might not understand it all now," they say, "but in the sweet by and by, we shall meet on that glorious shore. Oh, Lord God, prepare us a cabin in glory land."

Jesus did promise future glory when He said,

> *Do not let your hearts be troubled. Trust in God; trust also in me. In my Father's house are many rooms; if it were not so, I would have told you. I am going there to prepare a place for you. And if I go and prepare a place for you, I will come back and take you to be with me that you also may be where I am.*
>
> (John 14:1–3)

But Jesus also promised spiritual results for *today*, for the *here and now*:

> *I tell you the truth, anyone who has faith in me will do what*
> *I have been doing. He will do even greater things than these,*
> *because I am going to the Father.*   (John 14:12)

If we believe in Jesus, we should expect to see the same miracles He had in His ministry. We are to continue His ministry on the earth.

Jesus established the church based on His miracle-working power. A congregation that never experiences miracles is not the body of believers that Jesus established. Religion without the supernatural is dead. But our God is alive!

God hasn't changed. He still wants to bless His people. Jesus said that whoever has faith in Him *"will do even greater things than these, because I am going to the Father."* He promised *"greater things,"* not lesser things. We should expect and receive *"greater things."*

> WE SHOULD EXPECT TO SEE THE MIRACLES JESUS HAD IN HIS MINISTRY.

Jesus said, *"And I will do whatever you ask in my name, so that the Son may bring glory to the Father"* (verse 13). Did you catch that? *"Whatever you ask"*! That is a powerful promise, and I believe it.

Jesus said, *"You may ask me for anything in my name, and I will do it"* (verse 14). He said, *"Anything"*! Praise God! *"Anything"*! That is what our God has promised. He said, *"I will do it"* (emphasis added). What is this *"it"*? This *"it"* refers to *"anything"* we ask our heavenly Father in prayer.

In many religious settings, ministers are afraid to talk about the supernatural because it upsets some people. They don't like to hear about deliverance and healing. As a pastor, I cannot stop speaking about these things, no matter whom I offend. Sick people still need healing, bound people still need deliverance, and God is still in the business of healing and delivering. If that offends someone, I am sorry. I can't change it.

Jesus repeated the promise of John 14:14 a few chapters later when He said,

> *In that day you will no longer ask me anything. I tell you the truth, my Father will give you whatever you ask in my name. Until now you have not asked for anything in my name. Ask and you will receive, and your joy will be complete.*
> (John 16:23–24)

"Whatever"! What a powerful word! That is what God has promised to those of us who believe Him. He tells us to ask so that our *"joy will be complete."* He is concerned about our true needs. He doesn't want us to be without the fullness of joy.

And when we ask, we should expect to receive what we ask for. His promise is, *"You will receive."* What will we receive? We will receive *"whatever"* we ask in His name. This is God's promise. We should never be surprised when God works a miracle for us. We should expect to see the signs and wonders of God in our midst.

WE SHOULD NEVER BE SURPRISED WHEN GOD WORKS A MIRACLE FOR US.

Growing up in the simplicity of African life, it seemed to us the most logical thing to believe and receive what God had promised. And prayer and fasting played a crucial role in bringing those promises to pass.

WHEN PEOPLE FORGET
TO PRAY AND FAST

Later in life, I witnessed the tragedies of several people who forgot to pray, fast, and seek the face of God. What happened to them confirms in my mind and heart the necessity of prayer and fasting in each believer's life.

One story is about a very simple woman of prayer in Africa, for whom God did outstanding miracles. She had never attended seminary and had no college degree, but she was powerful in God. After she had spent time praying in a certain place, sick people who came there would be healed, and people with serious problems would be delivered.

When foreign missionaries came and saw what was happening in the life of this woman, they convinced her to travel with them throughout Europe and the United States. Unfortunately, they commercialized her gift, using her to raise money. Soon, her special anointing departed. She still weeps for those days, the days when God worked wonders through her, but they do not return. She forgot how to wait upon God in prayer and fasting, and she lost her anointing as a result.

Another example involved a man from Kenya who came to the United States. He had been used mightily of God in Kenya, but when he came to America, it wasn't long before the miracles ceased in his life and ministry. The lure of riches caused him to compromise his anointing. Later, he found it difficult to even remember the mighty things that God had done for him. They seemed like faraway dreams.

When he came to visit us, I felt led to ask him if he would join me in fasting for three days. He did, and at the end of that time, he told me what had happened to him and his anointing.

When he had arrived in America years ago, everyone offered him food. When he wanted to fast, his hosts objected, saying that it would be offensive to fast. "This is America," they said. "Enjoy our American hospitality. You can fast some other time." It was the same everywhere he went. Before long, he had given up his habit of regular fasting, and his anointing began to fade.

We must remember that we can maintain a simple faith in God and experience His miracles on a regular basis *only if we are dedicated to a life of prayer and fasting*. This is the reason, despite the fact that so many believers have abandoned the custom, that I still believe in prayer and fasting.

PART III

WHY PRAY AND FAST

INTRODUCTION
TO PART III

We live in a needy culture. How many times have you heard a child—your own or someone else's—tell his parents that he *needs* that new toy he just saw on TV? Or a young lady insist to her mother that she *needs* more new clothes because hers are so outdated?

Children aren't the only culprits either. Adults are just as guilty of saying that they *need* a new car or *need* a bigger house or *need* more money. I think it's safe to say that we live in a very, very needy, "gimme more" culture!

But what about the things we really need? Things like more faith, a closer relationship with God, an eternal perspective, and more power for our lives. These are the things that we *do* need, yet very few people are clamoring to get them.

Prayer and fasting puts us in a position to both desire these things and to receive them. Fasting is the key that unlocks the door to the things that we truly need. Do you need more power? More of God? More faith? Fasting holds the answers.

EIGHT

The Need to Crucify the Flesh

JAMES 4:1–3

What causes fights and quarrels among you? Don't they come from your desires that battle within you? You want something but don't get it. You kill and covet, but you cannot have what you want. You quarrel and fight. You do not have, because you do not ask God. When you ask, you do not receive, because you ask with wrong motives, that you may spend what you get on your pleasures.

THE NEED TO CRUCIFY THE FLESH

any people treat fasting like a tool to twist the arm of God. They think, "If I fast, God will give me what I want." The problem with this attitude is that flesh comes first. The fasting person's focus, in such a situation, is on his own fleshly needs and wants.

True fasting, however, crucifies the flesh. It gets your flesh out of the way so that the Spirit of God can move in your life. It removes the barriers to communication with God and allows the spirit-man to commune directly with the heavenly Father—without disturbance. When a person determines to truly fast, he or she determines to remove the obstacles preventing total submission to the will of God.

THE BATTLE FOR YOUR SOUL

Satan is determined to eradicate the practice of prayer and fasting. Why? Because fasting tears down his strongholds! Fasting clears the way for our victory, and the enemy will do anything to prevent that.

WHEN KINGS PRAY AND FAST

Satan wants you to be poor, to give free rein to your appetites until they consume you. The food industry, the illegal drug industry, and the entertainment industry have much in common: They all pander to the runaway appetites of our society. Much of today's poverty is a direct result of this almost total loss of control.

Most of us who live comfortably in prosperous nations have problems with prayer and fasting because everything around us appeals to our flesh and its carnal desires. But when we seek the face of God through prayer and fasting, we push the flesh aside, denying the appetites that seek to control us. We allow our spirit-man, who desires God, to develop a strong relationship with the heavenly Father.

> FASTING SETS YOUR SPIRIT FREE TO WORSHIP AND SERVE GOD.

Man is a triune being made up of body, soul, and spirit. It is the spirit that came from God and longs to be reunited with God. Given the opportunity, and once it is renewed by the Holy Spirit, a person's spirit-man will reach out to God and communicate with Him.

The three parts of a person, however, compete for influence. Your spirit can influence your soul, and your soul can influence your flesh. If your soul is magnifying the Lord, your flesh will bow in submission. If your flesh has risen to authority in your life, however, it will struggle with your spirit for dominance, and the soul will end up obeying the lusts of the flesh.

This is where fasting comes in. Fasting sets your spirit free to worship and serve God. It subdues the flesh so that the spirit can have control.

WHEN FLESH SNEAKS INTO OUR PRAYERS

In James 4, James gave two reasons that our prayers go unanswered: because we don't ask and because we ask with wrong motives.

> *From whence come wars and fightings among you? come they not hence, even of your lusts that war in your members? Ye lust, and have not: ye kill, and desire to have, and cannot obtain: ye fight and war, yet ye have not, because ye ask not. Ye ask, and receive not, because ye ask amiss, that ye may consume it upon your lusts.* (James 4:1–3 KJV)

To *"ask amiss"* is to ask with wrong motives, with fleshly desires, with carnal intent. It is when we pray for the wrong things and then *"consume* [them] *upon* [our] *lusts."*

Many of us are guilty of taking the blessings of God and "consuming them" upon our own lusts. Is it any wonder that we don't get immediate answers the next time we pray?

If you constantly live and work for the flesh, you will produce the works of flesh and death. If, however, you live and work in agreement with the Spirit of God, you will produce life.

Your flesh resists anything that will bring it into subjection. Your flesh doesn't want to fast because it wants to be in control. You must insist upon it or else be doomed to constant control by the flesh and the devil.

The flesh will use every imaginable excuse to keep you from fasting. A few of the more common ones are

- "You are not ready to fast."
- "Now is not the best time; wait until next week."

- "You don't have time to really seek the face of God right now, so you might as well wait for another opportunity."
- "You might offend other members of your family."

A word of warning: When you desire to fast and draw near to God, expect the enemy of your soul to fight in every way possible to prevent it. He doesn't want you to fast. At the very moment you decide to fast, he will present you with some irresistible invitation to eat out. He will tempt you with a food advertisement. He will cause you to remember all your favorite foods. He will bring up all kinds of obstacles that you never would have imagined. Be prepared for his wiles.

THE EXAMPLE OF OUR LORD

The God we serve is the same God who provided manna for the Israelites in the desert. When he came to earth as a man, He fed multitudes with a few loaves and fish. He easily could have turned stones into bread to satisfy His hunger in the desert, but He refused. (See Matthew 4:3–4.) He was determined to submit the flesh of Jesus of Nazareth, the man, to His heavenly Father so that He could have the power of God in His life. After this, when His period of prayer and fasting had ended, Jesus entered into a mighty ministry of deliverance and miracles. That same power is waiting for each of us who will dare to believe God, obey Him, and surrender our flesh to the Spirit.

WHEN GOD HAS TO SAY "NO"

Our prayers are not proper prayers when they are influenced by the flesh. James knew believers who were praying such prayers. As we saw earlier, they were asking *"amiss"* (James 4:3 KJV). Their motives were not good, and they were praying for selfish reasons.

THE NEED TO CRUCIFY THE FLESH

The Father, in love and mercy, had to refuse the requests of these believers. Why? Because He knows what is good for us, and He wants all the glory. When the flesh is seeking glory and fulfillment, God is forced to withhold His blessing. He cannot give the flesh any reason to glory.

For example, God cannot further bless many people on their jobs because, if He did, they would take all the credit for the things He's done. He wants *all* the glory, not just some of it. The flesh must be crucified for this to happen.

CRUCIFY THE FLESH

Get your flesh crucified so that God can get all the glory in your life. If you can get your flesh out of the way, your steps can be *"ordered by the LORD"* (Psalm 37:23 KJV). If you can get your flesh out of the way, the Spirit can have full liberty to do what He desires in and through you. If you can get your flesh out of the way, you will have more clarity about what to pray for and a greater sensitivity in the Spirit.

> GOD WANTS *ALL* THE GLORY, NOT JUST SOME OF IT.

When we are dominated by the flesh, however, we don't even know what to pray for. We think we know what we need, but we are so much like little children, desiring that which, many times, is actually harmful. When we get closer to God through prayer and fasting, though, we begin to realize what we *really* need. God knows what we need better than we do. He can show us what our priorities should be. He can also show us exactly how to go about receiving what we need.

WHEN KINGS PRAY AND FAST

A great example of this is King David. David became the anointed king of Israel because he learned the secret of getting his flesh out of the way so that God could work in him. David wrote, *"My knees are weak through fasting; and my flesh faileth of fatness"* (Psalms 109:24 KJV). He had weak knees from fasting, but this gave him a strong spirit.

When we crucify the flesh and discipline the body, our spirits become useful instruments for God. Fasting removes the weaknesses in your life and leaves you strong to face life's battles. Paul learned that lesson well. He stayed in the presence of God until he received the answer he needed.

> *But I keep under my body, and bring it into subjection: lest that by any means, when I have preached to others, I myself should be a castaway.* (1 Corinthians 9:27 KJV)

WHEN WE CRUCIFY THE FLESH, OUR SPIRITS BECOME USEFUL INSTRUMENTS.

Fasting also helps us to bring every thought into obedience to Christ. Fasting enables us to conquer the evil thoughts of our carnal minds. It helps us to "cast down" the *"imaginations, and every high thing that exalteth itself against the knowledge of God"* (2 Corinthians 10:5 KJV).

When the flesh is controlled, the prayer life can thrive. Paul taught about experiences in prayer that, unfortunately, very few people have these days. He called us to

> *pray in the Spirit on all occasions with all kinds of prayers and requests. With this in mind, be alert and always keep on praying for all the saints.* (Ephesians 6:18)

The Need to Crucify the Flesh

When Paul said to pray *"all kinds of prayers"* (Ephesians 6:18), he was calling us to employ every method available to us in prayer. Many of us have been taught only one method of prayer: the "anguish" method. By this I mean that many people only call on God in extreme emergencies, when they are in deep trouble. Those who go no further in their prayer life never learn how to praise God effectively. Yet Jesus taught us that the very first thing we are to do in prayer is to give Him the glory and the honor He deserves: *"Our Father in heaven, hallowed be your name"* (Matthew 6:9).

Many people take their long wish lists into their periods of prayer and fasting. They never wait on God for His wisdom, His knowledge, and His understanding. They are too busy asking Him for things.

If we are still in the "what-can-I-get?" mode, we are still carnal, still living by the flesh, and not spiritual at all. God is not looking for opportunists; He is looking for people who love and appreciate Him and want to build a relationship with Him.

> THE SPIRIT OF CHRIST IS ONE OF GIVING, NOT OF GETTING.

He wants people who love Him for Him—not because of what they can get in return.

It is not wrong to receive things from God. There are many things we need, and He wants to supply our needs. But the Spirit of Christ is not a spirit of getting; it is a spirit of giving. For this reason the Scriptures declare,

God loves a cheerful giver.   (2 Corinthians 9:7)

Before we start thinking about what we need from God, there are some things we can give to Him first. Start your prayers by giving Him your heart and your praise. This will help you as you continue to crucify your flesh.

One thing is sure: Fasting will never take you down. When you develop a regular habit of fasting, you can only go upward spiritually.

Your flesh will complain. It will say that it is dying, that it is becoming ugly, that it is sick and weak. Don't give in to the flesh. Instead, submit to the Spirit of God. You want the flesh to die, and you will never be sorry that you crucified the flesh. The promise of the Scriptures is that *"the mind of sinful man is death, but the mind controlled by the Spirit is life and peace"* (Romans 8:6).

Use prayer and fasting as a tool—not to twist God's arm but rather to deal your flesh a deathblow.

NINE

The Need to Hear the Voice of God

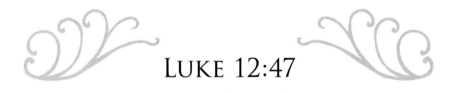

LUKE 12:47

That servant who knows his master's
will and does not get ready or does
not do what his master wants will be
beaten with many blows.

THE NEED TO HEAR THE VOICE OF GOD

B ecause Christ is our Lord and Savior, and because we are totally dependent on Him, it is of the utmost importance that we know His will at any given time. Unfortunately, this is the area where many believers fail—because to know the will of God, it is necessary to live close to Him and hear His voice first.

Prayer and fasting makes you sensitive to the voice of the Lord. It enables you to hear Him above the din of other voices around you. What could be more important than hearing the voice of the Almighty God?

Once you hear the voice of God, you can also start seeing His hand. But you have to hear Him first. If you don't hear the voice of God, it will be difficult to see the hand of God! And one of the best ways to hear the voice of God is by practicing prayer and fasting.

SEEK YE FIRST

As believers, every decision we make should be inspired by God. Every move should be ordained by Him. If our actions are not inspired by God and in accordance with His will for our lives, we have no guarantee of success in what we do. As Jesus said, *"Seek ye first the kingdom of God, and his righteousness; and all these things shall be added unto you"* (Matthew 6:33 KJV).

> FORTUNATELY, GOD ISN'T PLAYING "HIDE-AND-SEEK" WITH US.

Fortunately, God isn't playing "hide-and-seek" with us. He is not trying to disguise His will or make it some mystery we have to solve. He wants to be able to communicate with us anytime about what He wants for our lives. But for this to work, we must seek Him:

*Ask and it will be given to you; **seek** and you will find; knock and the door will be opened to you.*
(Matthew 7:7, emphasis added)

*God did this so that men would **seek** him and perhaps reach out for him and find him, though he is not far from each one of us.* (Acts 17:27, emphasis added)

*If ye then be risen with Christ, **seek** those things which are above, where Christ sitteth on the right hand of God.*
(Colossians 3:1 KJV, emphasis added)

***Seek** the LORD while he may be found; call on him while he is near.* (Isaiah 55:6, emphasis added)

When we seek the Lord, He promises to be found by us.

*You will **seek** me and find me when you seek me with all your heart.* (Jeremiah 29:13, emphasis added)

SEEKING AND FASTING—
LIKE TWO PEAS IN A POD

Seeking the Lord and fasting go hand in hand. How? Well, it is difficult to seek the Lord *"with all your heart"* (Jeremiah 29:13) when you have a full stomach.

Sometimes we desire to hear from God, but the flesh wants to do its own thing. It tells us,

- "Change into something more comfortable!"
- "Get a cool drink from the refrigerator and something to snack on!"
- "Lie down on the couch and take a nap!"
- "Just relax! Get comfy!"

Before long we are snoring, and all thoughts of seeking God are lost. When we fast, however, the spirit-man is nourished as the flesh is denied. We can truly seek with our whole hearts when the flesh has been silenced and stilled.

FASTING SHARPENS YOUR SIGHT

Those who never fast rarely see visions or have spiritual dreams. When we fast and wait in the presence of God, however, He will speak to us in many different ways. Often He will put a word in our spirits, or He will give a vision or a dream. Sometimes He will speak to us through circumstances, nature, experiences, or preaching.

The bottom line is this: When you fast, God *will* speak to you, in one way or another. Don't stop fasting until you have heard from God.

When I fast, I expect to hear from God. I expect Him to reveal Himself to me in a greater way. I expect to receive the specific instruction I need for my personal life and for my ministry. I expect Him to correct me in the areas where I am lacking and to show me things about the future. He never fails me.

GOD IS ANXIOUSLY WAITING TO REVEAL MANY THINGS TO US.

It is not wrong to expect answers to your prayers. When I talk to God, I expect Him to respond because:

(1) I know that He hears me, and

(2) I know that He answers me.

He is anxiously waiting to reveal many things to us; we must only dedicate ourselves to a time of seeking Him.

THE BEST WAY TO KNOW HIS WILL

Knowing the will of God is the greatest struggle most believers face in life. They ask themselves such questions as,

- "Is it God's will for me to get married?"
- "Is this the right person for me?"
- "Is it God's will for me to go into business?"
- "Should I go into the ministry?"

These are all important questions. Knowing and obeying God's will for our lives means the difference between success and failure. We desperately need to know His perfect will for today, and we could avoid so many tragedies in life if we were more conscious of what God wanted.

Most decisions in Western society—be they political, social, spiritual, economical, or educational—are made around a dining room table. Imagine the impact we could make if all our plans were made around dedicated prayer and fasting instead!

THE NEED TO HEAR THE VOICE OF GOD

The only way to really know God's will is to get the flesh pushed aside long enough to hear His voice, to discover His heart. That, in itself, is sufficient reason for concerted prayer and fasting.

TEN

The Need
for Power

MATTHEW 4:1–2

Then Jesus was led by the Spirit
into the desert to be tempted by the devil.
After fasting forty days and forty nights,
he was hungry.

THE NEED FOR POWER

Many congregations rightly devote their attention to seeing sinners get saved and come to a saving knowledge of Christ. Unfortunately, though, this is as far as some churches go. Often, very little is done to ensure that new converts receive anointing from the Holy Spirit so that they become effective for the kingdom of God.

In a sense, we abandon them. Once they are born again, we leave them as powerless infants, helpless against the evil intents of the enemy. This is not God's plan for His church.

God's desire is for His church to be made up of bold, power-filled believers. Believers who are strong. Believers who walk in victory. Believers who mirror the power Christ displayed in His own life.

OUR EXAMPLE

Jesus is our example. While He was here on earth, He showed amazing power, power that we are to demonstrate as well.

One of the greatest examples of power was the compassion he showed in His life. Many people, when looking for a church home, think first of "friendliness" and a "loving environment."

While it is good to look for loving people, we must remember that true love, the love of God, is only manifested through His power. True love shows itself in action. This is what compassion is all about.

Everyone has a measure of love, even people of the world. Godly love, or compassion, however, is another level of love the world can never hope to attain.

GOD WANTS HIS CHURCH TO BE MADE UP OF POWER-FILLED BELIEVERS.

To see the importance of compassion, just look at Jesus' life here on earth. His ministry was so effective, so powerful, because He was *"moved with compassion"* over and over again. Just look at how many times Christ's compassion led Him to loving displays of power.

*But when he saw the multitudes, he was moved with **compassion** on them, because they fainted, and were scattered abroad, as sheep having no shepherd.*
(Matthew 9:36 KJV, emphasis added)

*And Jesus went forth, and saw a great multitude, and was moved with **compassion** toward them, and he healed their sick.*
(Matthew 14:14 KJV, emphasis added)

*Jesus called his disciples to him and said, "I have **compassion** for these people; they have already been with me three days and have nothing to eat. I do not want to send them away hungry, or they may collapse on the way."*
(Matthew 15:32, emphasis added)

*Jesus had **compassion** on them and touched their eyes. Immediately they received their sight and followed him.*
(Matthew 20:34, emphasis added)

THE NEED FOR POWER

*Filled with **compassion**, Jesus reached out his hand and touched the man. "I am willing," he said. "Be clean!"*

(Mark 1:41, emphasis added)

Jesus was moved with compassion, and this manifested itself in power. We need to be showing this same power and compassion in our churches today. Unfortunately, some congregations have missed the boat.

POWERLESSNESS IN THE PEWS...
AND THE PULPIT

Be aware: Not all believers who claim to be loving have genuine compassion, and not all believers who claim to be powerful really have power.

One reason we don't see more miraculous demonstrations of God's power these days is because we have religious entertainers in the pulpit instead of power-filled preaching to God's people.

Ministers have been trained to be eloquent orators, and they tell us some very nice things—usually just what we want to hear. After listening to several soothing sermons, we become complacent and stop seeking God's best for our lives.

Politicians have always been skilled at putting a certain "spin" on things so that they become acceptable. Those who work in the news media frequently do the same. Sadly, many preachers are now learning this tactic. You can now sit in weekly services and never feel uncomfortable, never feel challenged. Such pastors make you feel totally satisfied with your present position in God. This is surely the day of which Amos prophesied:

"The days are coming," declares the Sovereign LORD, "when I will send a famine through the land—not a famine of food or a

thirst for water, but a famine of hearing the words of the LORD. Men will stagger from sea to sea and wander from north to east, searching for the word of the LORD, but they will not find it. In that day the lovely young women and strong young men will faint because of thirst." (Amos 8:11–13)

THE PRICE OF POWER

The lack of power in our lives doesn't mean that there is a lack of want. People today are hungry for power, and some will travel long distances in search of the true, power-filled Word of the Lord. Because these people are hungry for something more real, challenging, and transforming, it is not uncommon for people to drive sixty miles to church or to go halfway across the country for a special conference. God's Word is being performed, and people are hungry for the supernatural.

> PEOPLE TODAY ARE HUNGRY FOR POWER AND WILL TRAVEL FAR TO FIND IT.

Unfortunately, many people's hunger for the supernatural has led them to look outside the things of God. Because they don't see power in believers' lives, many people are turning to Eastern religions and New Age thinking. Hungry people are susceptible to deceit.

Many of these devilish practices have even been adopted by corporate America in the guise of "productivity training." Outlandish practices are taught in seminars sponsored by the corporations in our country. Many false prophets have entered into the world, and many people are being deceived. In turn, they then go on to deceive others.

The Need for Power

Many ministers are preaching more like civil rights activists these days than men of deliverance. There is no power in their message, no anointing in their hands, and nothing is happening under their leadership. Many of them are good people. They are handsome, intelligent, and caring. But they have lost the power of God. What do they have to offer?

Most of us are impressed by good preaching. "He is a good preacher," we say or, "She is a good communicator. She knows how to get her point across." But where are the miracles? Where is the power of God? It is one thing to have a silver tongue and another thing to see and experience the power of God on a regular basis. Preaching can be entertaining and yet empty. It can be pleasant to the ears and yet void of power.

Intellect doesn't cast out devils. If it did, we would be calling upon professors, not pastors, to deliver people who are tormented. Men and women of power, whatever their status in life, are the ones God uses to drive away evil spirits and bring healing.

The church of the Lord Jesus Christ is being called back to the basics, to apply itself seriously to battle. We must return to the simple gospel, to the power of God that enables us to stand against any enemy.

No amount of funding or reeducation can stop this trend toward the occult. The only hope is for God's people to rise up in indignation and take control of the situation.

What's the Answer?

The only hope of reversing the gains of the enemy is through concerted prayer and fasting. Prayer and fasting opens the door to true spiritual power like nothing else.

According to Matthew 4:1–2, Jesus was *"led by the Spirit into the desert,"* and it was there that He fasted *"forty days and forty nights."* He didn't go there to be seen by men. He didn't go there to fulfill some tradition of his fathers. He went there to get the power of God in His life; and when He came forth from that solitary place, no enemy could stand against Him. He was powerful.

> *God anointed Jesus of Nazareth with the Holy Spirit and power, and...he went around doing good and healing all who were under the power of the devil, because God was with him.* (Acts 10:38)

When Jesus returned to the synagogue in Nazareth, He was accorded the honor of a visitor and given the privilege of reading the Scriptures in public. He read from Isaiah 61:1–2:

> *The Spirit of the Lord is on me, because he has anointed me to preach good news to the poor. He has sent me to proclaim freedom for the prisoners and recovery of sight for the blind, to release the oppressed, to proclaim the year of the Lord's favor.* (Luke 4:18–19)

When He had finished the reading, Jesus said to the congregation: *"This day is this scripture fulfilled in your ears"* (Luke 4:21 KJV). Waiting upon God the Father in prayer and fasting had placed a special anointing upon the life of Jesus, and that special anointing enabled Him to do the works of God. Prayer and fasting can open the door to power in our lives today, as well. And, oh, how we need the power of God in our churches today!

SOME REAL-LIFE EXAMPLES

For more than thirty-five years, I have lived for the Word of God. Nothing else is more important to me. It works, I can rely on it, and it never fails. I can preach it without reservation. Therefore, I am unwilling to preach the theory of the Word while never seeing its power in action. I want to see the Word at work. I want to see the power of God transforming lives. I have no interest in playing games. I am angry with the devil, and I am determined not to give him a single inch.

> I HAVE NO INTEREST IN PLAYING GAMES; I WANT TO SEE THE POWER OF GOD.

I thank God for the miracles I have experienced in my ministry. On eight different occasions I have seen the dead raised. (And I don't mean people who fainted. I mean people without breath—dead people.) God's power brought them back to life.

Many people, even religious leaders, would say things like:

- That's impossible.
- Things like that don't happen anymore.
- That type of miracle passed away with the apostolic age.
- When the disciples died, their gifts died with them.
- We cannot expect to see what the apostles saw.

And yet, I have seen cripples walk, just as the original apostles did. I have seen blind eyes opened, just as the apostles did. I have seen the deaf and dumb healed, just as the disciples did. I have watched God heal open sores right before my eyes. And it all came because I fasted and prayed, just as the apostles did.

One man I prayed for was so mentally ill he had to be chained to a tree. His name was Yeboah, but many referred to him as "the wild animal." Left loose, he recklessly destroyed lives and property. He was so possessed that he ate his own excrement. On several occasions he received supernatural strength and was able to snap the chains that held him. No medicine could sedate him. But I saw him delivered through prayer and fasting. God's power is greater than any other, and we can tap into that power through prayer and fasting.

Prayer and fasting will open your spirit to the supernatural. I am convinced that most of the miracles, healings, and signs and wonders we see in our ministry result from prayer and fasting. Because of that, fasting is not a heavy burden for me. It is a joy. How could I not fast? While some look forward to a good meal, I look forward to the opportunity to shut myself away with God, without distraction, in order to draw closer to my heavenly Father.

Any congregation that has not learned to pray and fast will not have an effective demonstration of the gifts of the Spirit, which are demonstrations of God's power in our midst. Much of what is passing as gifts of the Spirit these days, the prophecies and words of knowledge, are ineffective because many of the people prophesying or giving the words of knowledge have not spent time with God. Their words are shallow. Some who are calling themselves "prophets" have never fasted more than a few hours at a time. They only fast between meals. How could they know the mind of God if they have not taken time out to seek it?

> PRAYER AND FASTING OPENS YOUR SPIRIT TO THE SUPERNATURAL.

Some people who give a word of knowledge change their minds two or three times before they finally get it out. But God doesn't speak that way. He speaks in specifics. Those people need to do more fasting and praying. God can tell you exactly what's wrong with a person; He can tell you where they live; He can tell you what they like to eat. Let God be specific. Look for a community of believers where genuine gifts—genuine demonstrations of God's power—are in evidence.

TIME FOR A CHANGE

If your spiritual needs are not being met by your minister, it is time to shake the dust from your feet and go where you can be fed, where God's power is in demonstration. I understand that such a move is not always easy. People are reluctant to move from one congregation to another for many reasons.

"My grandmother grew up in this congregation," they say. They have a lot of friends in their Sunday school. And will another church be any better?

I understand these reservations. But don't stay in a dead congregation just because your grandparents were members there. Find one that means business for God. Your soul and the souls of your other family members are at stake. Look for local body where people love Jesus enough to seek His face and present His Word in power and glory. Look for a place that has more than a few minutes of prayer at a time. Look for a place where fasting is taught and practiced. In every congregation, those who have serious positions of ministry should be required to fast. Look for a place where this is the case.

An old African proverbs says, "A dead hen cannot hatch fresh eggs." Put good eggs under a dead hen and the eggs will die, too. Something dead cannot give life. Something powerless cannot generate power.

Without prayer and fasting, you cannot see the gospel's "bottom line." You cannot have God's very best for your life. You cannot experience all that He has promised. The promises of God are not for the carnal. They are not for those who walk in the flesh. They are reserved for those who walk in the Spirit.

Because of its importance, Jesus made fasting a requirement for us. He said,

> *How can the guests of the bridegroom mourn while he is with them? The time will come when the bridegroom will be taken from them; then they will fast.* (Matthew 9:15)

Considering their lack of prayer and fasting, it is no wonder that most congregations rarely see a miracle. It is no wonder that the power of God is never manifested in their midst. God's power comes to those who seek Him. It is time to start seeking Him through prayer and fasting.

ELEVEN

The Need
for More Faith

HEBREWS 4:1–3

Therefore, since the promise of entering his rest still stands,
let us be careful that none of you be found to have
fallen short of it. For we also have had the gospel
preached to us, just as they did; but the message they heard
was of no value to them, because those who heard
did not combine it with faith. Now we who have believed
enter that rest, just as God has said, "So I declared on oath
in my anger, 'They shall never enter my rest.'"
And yet his work has been finished
since the creation of the world.

THE NEED FOR MORE FAITH

G od has given promises to His people down through the centuries. When these promises are believed, amazing things happen. When these promises are not believed, however, when the Word is not *"combine*[d]*...with faith,"* there is no result. God's blessings are not automatic. The Word must be *"combine*[d]*...with faith"* to produce God's blessings in our lives.

One of these blessings is rest. Those who believe the Word of God enter into His rest. That means that if you receive the Word of God and walk by faith, you will always have rest in the Lord. Nothing will disturb your peace. Nothing will perturb you. Those who do not walk by faith, however, will live in constant turmoil and confusion.

As you can see, nothing is more important to our lives than our faith. We are saved by faith. We are healed by faith. We receive miracles by faith. We receive and operate the gifts of the Spirit by faith. Everything we do is by faith. And, as we have already seen,

> *without faith it is impossible to please God, because anyone who comes to him must believe that he exists and that he rewards those who earnestly seek him.* (Hebrews 11:6)

BY FAITH, NOT BY SIGHT

God is pleased when we believe Him. He is pleased when we walk by faith in Him, not by what we can readily see with our eyes.

God loves us and wants the very best for us. Everything He does is for our benefit. Our faith in His goodness sets in motion the forces of the universe. We can have faith in Him, knowing that He understands what we're going through:

> *For we do not have a high priest who is unable to sympathize with our weaknesses, but we have one who has been tempted in every way, just as we are—yet was without sin. Let us then approach the throne of grace with confidence, so that we may receive mercy and find grace to help us in our time of need.*
>
> (Hebrews 4:15–16)

As this verse reminds us, Jesus is our High Priest. He took His own shed blood into the presence of God and made a new covenant with us through it. Now, because of Him, we are covered with His blood and can come *"with confidence"* into His presence.

OUR FAITH IS NOT BASED ON WHAT WE SEE WITH OUR PHYSICAL EYES.

Our faith is not based on what we see. We must accept by faith what we cannot readily glimpse with our physical eyes. Airplanes often leave a white trail in the sky. Sometimes we can see this trail, but we can't see the airplane itself. It is the same in the believer's life. Sometimes we can see the results of God working in our lives but may not be able to see the Lord Himself with our physical eyes. Yet we know He is always there. We accept it by faith.

FAITH IS FILLED WITH HOPE

We need to wake up each morning with faith for a wonderful day. We need to walk in faith that God is watching out for us and that everything will be done for our good. We need to go to God in faith, believing that He will meet us and touch us in the area of our need.

Many people go to their church with serious problems. They listen to the preaching or the teaching but are unable to take advantage of what they are hearing. The message goes in one ear and out the other. They cannot appropriate it.

The problem is not that Jesus doesn't understand the situation. He does. He was tempted in every way. He is able to deal with any and every situation. There is no conceivable problem that is too great for Him.

FAITH ISN'T JUST SOME MENTAL ASSENT; IT IS A WAY OF LIFE.

The problem is not that He doesn't understand; it's that we don't believe. We need to believe Him. We need to get our mind on Him and talk to Him—in faith.

FAITH IN ACTION

Paul wrote to the Romans,

For therein is the righteousness of God revealed from faith to faith: as it is written, The just shall live by faith.
(Romans 1:17 KJV)

"The just shall live by faith." Faith isn't just some mental assent; it is a way of life. Faith affects everything we do. It makes us walk

WHEN KINGS PRAY AND FAST

right and talk right. *"The just shall live by faith"* (Romans 1:17 KJV). The faith of the just will produce the proper works. Because they believe, they will act on that belief.

> *In the same way, faith by itself, if it is not accompanied by action, is dead.* (James 2:17)

FAITH THAT DOESN'T PRODUCE IS MEANINGLESS.

A person who doesn't put his faith to work is like a man who has lost his job. He may have many abilities, but he will soon go bankrupt because he is not working.

A corporation may have a name and a legal status, but if it produces nothing and accomplishes nothing, it will soon falter.

In the same way, faith that doesn't produce is meaningless. It is dead.

POSITIVE AND NEGATIVE FAITH

Most believers have faith of some sort, but their faith is either barely breathing or it's a negative faith.

Faith works in two directions. There is a positive faith, and there is a negative faith. They are equally powerful.

What is negative faith? Many believers expect all the worst things to happen to them—and they usually do. This is negative faith.

Let your faith be positive. Let it produce the appropriate action. If you aren't willing to get up in the morning and put forth an effort to support your family, you soon won't have a family to support. You can wake up every morning and quote dozens of Scriptures, but if you do nothing, your faith is vain. It accomplishes nothing. Action, however, pleases God. It proves your faith.

The Need for More Faith

Positive faith in action also displeases Satan. The enemy knows whether we believe or not. He knows whether we depend on God or not. He knows if we spend time with the heavenly Father or not. He knows if we wait in the presence of God for power and authority over him or not.

Are you pleasing God and displeasing Satan? Or do you have it the other way around?

Fasting and Faith

When we spend time with the Father, our faith grows. The better we know Him and the more we know about His power and glory, the more our faith grows. Because we know more about the Lord, we have more faith in Him and in His Word.

One of the best ways to know the Lord better is to spend time with Him in prayer and fasting. Satan trembles when we pray and fast because he knows that we are receiving faith to cast down his kingdom. He hates fasting! He will do anything to keep us from obeying God in prayer and fasting. *Anything!*

Satan wants us to have weakened faith. He knows that if we don't mix the Word with faith, nothing will happen. He knows that if we don't pray with faith, our prayers will not be answered—and that if we *do* pray with faith, our prayers *will* be answered.

If you believe, you will receive whatever you ask for in prayer.
(Matthew 21:22, emphasis added)

Everything is possible for him who believes.
(Mark 9:23, emphasis added)

I tell you the truth, if anyone says to this mountain, "Go, throw yourself into the sea," and does not doubt in his heart but believes that what he says will happen, it will be done for him. Therefore

*I tell you, whatever you ask for in prayer, **believe** that you have received it, and it will be yours.*

(Mark 11:23–24, emphasis added)

*Then Jesus said to the centurion, "Go! It will be done **just as you believed it would**." And his servant was healed at that very hour.* (Matthew 8:13, emphasis added)

Satan knows that if we don't believe, we will not be healed and delivered from his afflictions. Satan wants, more than anything, *to keep us from believing.*

FAITH WITH FASTING CREATES POTENT PRAYER

Jesus taught us to pray always and to pray with faith. He taught us to pray the will of God for our lives and not to pray amiss (Luke 23:41 KJV).

But even then, many prayers will not be answered without fasting.

> MORE THAN ANYTHING, SATAN WANTS TO KEEP US FROM BELIEVING.

Think of Hannah, from the Old Testament. She desperately wanted a son and believed that it was God's will to give her one. She promised God that if He would bless her with such a child, she would dedicate him to serve the Lord. She fasted and prayed and believed God for the miracle. And God responded to her exercise of faith. (See 1 Samuel 1.)

Or think of Peter. When Peter was cast into prison, he was constantly guarded by four soldiers. His enemies intended to kill him as soon as Passover ended because he was causing too much trouble preaching about Jesus Christ and His miracles.

But before they could do that, something unusual happened. The angel of the Lord visited that prison. He woke Peter up and told him to get his sandals on. Then he led him out past the guards. The gate opened of its own accord, and Peter was set free.

This all happened because believers were gathered and praying. It was late at night, and no doubt many of them were sleepy. They could have been home in bed getting a good night's rest, but they had dedicated themselves to intercede for Peter.

When he was released from prison, Peter went straight to the house where he knew believers would be gathered praying. Sure enough, when he arrived, he heard them still praying.

Faith empowered by prayer and fasting is powerful. When we pray, are we expecting God to answer? Are we expecting something to happen? Are we looking for the miracle that God will do? Prayer and fasting sharpens your expectancy so that, when you ask, you expect to receive.

TWELVE

The Need
for Preparation

MATTHEW 7:24–27

Therefore everyone who hears these
words of mine and puts them into practice is like a
wise man who built his house on the rock. The rain
came down, the streams rose, and the winds blew and
beat against that house; yet it did not fall, because
it had its foundation on the rock. But everyone who hears
these words of mine and does not put them into practice is
like a foolish man who built his house on sand. The rain
came down, the streams rose, and the winds blew and
beat against that house, and it fell with a great crash.

THE NEED FOR PREPARATION

A wise man builds on the rock. His house is powerful. It can withstand any storm. In this same parable, a foolish man builds on the sand. His house is not well supported, and when storms come, his house falls.

Jesus was telling us, in this parable, about the need for a proper foundation. We need to build our lives on Jesus Christ, and we also need to prepare for the challenges life might bring. We must be people of preparation.

Some people will ask, "Why doesn't God hear my prayers?" Lack of faith may be one reason, but it's not the only reason. Lack of preparation is often the problem. Nothing is more important than preparation, yet many neglect to prepare themselves for life's challenges—and for Jesus' answers to their prayers regarding those challenges.

PREPARATION: A PREREQUISITE FOR SUCCESS

A student cannot depend on faith alone when exam day arrives. He or she must prepare for that exam, as well. It's the same in the spiritual realm. When a person is unprepared, it shows—regardless of how much faith he or she might have.

We've learned the importance of preparation in many realms, but we still haven't fully learned it in the spiritual realm. In the business world, for instance, successful people are always prepared people. A few poorly prepared people might obtain a degree of success, but such success is rarely lasting.

Preparation is crucial in the military, as well. There are no shortcuts. Soldiers who are not well prepared do not last long in time of war. When the enemy first attacks, they are easily defeated. They must be prepared.

Or think about athletes. The training to which they submit themselves should inspire us all. They train many hours a day. Some professional football players lift weights for four hours every day, just to toughen themselves up. And they not only train physically; they train themselves mentally and emotionally, as well.

We all recognize the importance of preparation. If you have any doubt about this, consider the following questions:

- Would you like to go to a doctor who was not well prepared?
- Would you like to cross a long bridge designed by an engineer who was not well prepared?
- Would you like your taxes to be done by an accountant who was not well prepared?

WHAT HAPPENS WHEN PREPARATION IS NEGLECTED

Preparation is essential for success. And often, lack of it can yield disastrous results. Yet, despite the fact that many realize the importance of preparation, a lot of people are neglecting it in their own lives.

How many recognize, for instance, that it is impossible to be a good husband or a good wife without preparation? How many know that it is impossible to be a good father or a good mother without being prepared?

Many men in America are being destroyed. Increasing numbers are in prison or involved in illegal activities. The reason they are failing is that they haven't set goals to work toward, and they don't seem to realize the importance of preparation.

> A LOT OF PEOPLE NEGLECT PREPARATION IN THEIR OWN LIVES.

Because so many men are failing, women have to take on more responsibility for the family. And when they have to work outside the home, the children are often neglected. As a result, too many children are not taking their studies seriously enough—all because their father was not well prepared for life and was thus a poor example.

WHY PREPARATION IS NEGLECTED

Preparation is not a pleasant word to most of us. It speaks of time and effort, both of which we don't want to "waste." It is true that preparation takes time; it is true that preparation takes effort. But everything worthwhile in life takes time and effort. If it's not worth the time and effort, it's probably not worth having.

Our society is one that looks for shortcuts. We cook by microwave. We travel by high-speed jets. We communicate by e-mail. We want to learn everything in a few easy steps or from a "how-to" manual. Nobody wants to do homework anymore. Nobody wants to put in the time necessary to excel. We don't like the sound of the word *preparation* because it precludes any shortcuts.

Believers are no different. We want to receive Bible results, but we don't want to pay the Bible price. We are always looking for shortcuts. We want to be blessed, but we don't want to do what is necessary to get that blessing. So we serve God when we feel like it. We serve God when it is convenient. We serve God when it seems to fit into our overall scheme of life. Or we serve Him only when we need Him. Otherwise, we either don't have the time or don't have the energy to dedicate to His purpose.

WHY PREPARATION IS
CRUCIAL TO BELIEVERS

As a believer, if you are unprepared, your life is in danger. You are subject to constant attack by the enemy of your soul. He sees you as an easy target because you are not prepared for his attacks.

IF YOU ARE UNPREPARED, YOUR LIFE IS IN DANGER.

Time spent in preparation is not time wasted. Preparation enables you to accomplish your purpose in life. If you are not prepared, you will fail.

How do we prepare ourselves in the spiritual realm? By reading God's Word and regularly spending time with Him in prayer and fasting. When you pray and fast, you heighten your spiritual discernment. You start to understand the Word of God better and know how to apply it to your life. Prayer and fasting is crucial to preparation in the spiritual realm.

THE NEED FOR PREPARATION

It took me nearly twenty-four years to understand why I had power and authority over the works of the enemy. There is no demon anywhere—in Africa, in India, in South America, in the United States, in Europe—that can defeat me if I maintain my relationship with God through prayer and fasting. All of them put together cannot defeat me. They can attack me, but they cannot win. And you can tell them I said so! They know where I live, but I am confident that, in Christ, I have the victory. That's how powerful a force prayer and fasting is in my life!

I have the assurance of spiritual victory just as certainly as I have the assurance of salvation. I know, beyond any shadow of a doubt, that I am saved. No one can convince me otherwise. I am confident in the Word of God and what it promises. Nobody can tell me that I am not saved. In the same way, and to the same degree, nothing can change my mind as to my authority and power over the works of the enemy. As a prepared believer who practices prayer and fasting, I know where I stand, and I can boldly state my case.

PREPARATION IN THE MINISTRY

Ministers of the gospel need to be well prepared. Many don't want to make the effort or spend the time to prepare themselves fully. When God gives them a ministerial gift, they think that means they have nothing at all to do, but this isn't the case. They need to prepare for the ministry to which God has called them. Some try to launch out into their ministry before they are ready, and they fail because they put the proverbial cart before the horse. If you're being called into the ministry, take time to sit and be trained. Don't get impatient.

One minister, whom I recognize as an outstanding teacher, has been affiliated with my ministry for many years. He realized the importance of preparation and submitted himself to training for some time. He didn't leap ahead of God.

Another minister I know quite well is so full of God that I love to hear him preach. If you have any discouragement at all, you just have to get close to him and your discouragement will vanish. He is that kind of man. Yet, for a period of time, he went everywhere with me in training.

Unfortunately, not everyone is as wise as these men were. Some people can't sit still for any time at all. They want to go out and change the world now. That's fine, but you can't change the world if you are not prepared.

> GOD DOESN'T HONOR LONE RANGERS IN HIS KINGDOM.

The Lone Ranger was a popular TV hero in his day, but God doesn't honor Lone Rangers in His kingdom. He wants prepared people who are willing to submit to training under others. Whatever your particular gift is, whatever your vocation in life, let God prepare you for the days ahead.

As a pastor and professor, I cannot stand in front of my congregation or my college class and expect to feed my people if I have not prepared myself. How can I give something I do not have? What would you think if your mother called you to the dinner table but forgot to prepare anything for the meal? What a crazy thought! It's just as crazy to try to do God's work without proper preparation.

TAKE THE OFFENSIVE

Some people seem to get by with little preparation until they experience a crisis. When they are attacked by the enemy, they don't know how to react properly because they have not prepared.

THE NEED FOR PREPARATION

Such people take a defensive stance at everything because they have never been trained at offense. In sports, defense is important, but the teams that ultimately take the top prizes also excel at offense. They are extremely well prepared.

When God called me to preach the gospel, I knew I had to prepare. I remember telling my mother what God had laid on my heart. She had wanted me to become an engineer.

I spent most of my vacation time that year preaching, and I loved it, but I decided not to drop out of college. I would finish college and do it for the Lord.

I knew my purpose in life. I knew my destiny. I knew that I had a message for my generation. But I was determined to give God my best, and that meant finishing school. Even though I could have neglected preparation and just jumped straight into the ministry, I refused to quit. I was going to finish school.

> DEFENSE IS IMPORTANT, BUT WE ALSO HAVE TO EXCEL AT OFFENSE.

If any man on the continent of Africa wanted to serve God, it was me. If any man was willing to believe God's Word, it was me. If any man was anxious to preach that Word, it was me. But I was also willing to pay any price to prepare for the Lord's work.

The day I graduated, I packed my bag and set out to start a little church in someone's single-stall garage in a little village. I lived right there in that stall. I put a blanket over two wooden benches, and that was my bed. I stayed there for a year. I wasn't afraid to take chances for God. My heart was prepared. My mind was prepared. And I was willing to pay the price.

When Kings Pray and Fast
The Privilege of Prayer
and Fasting

Prayer and fasting is an important element in any spiritual preparation, whether it be for life or for ministry. Jesus was well prepared to live as an example of the true Christian life, and He was well prepared for the ministry entrusted to Him by His Father. Because He had waited in the presence of the Father, He could boldly say,

The Spirit of the Lord is on me, because he has anointed me to preach good news to the poor. He has sent me to proclaim freedom for the prisoners and recovery of sight for the blind, to release the oppressed, to proclaim the year of the Lord's favor.

(Luke 4:18–19)

I thank God for the privilege of prayer and fasting. After more than thirty-nine years, I am still preparing myself. I haven't arrived. God is still working on me. Every day holds new challenges for me, and the greatest days are still ahead.

And while God is preparing me for greater things ahead in life, He is preparing me for the eternal life ahead, as well. Remember, life itself is preparation for something greater, for the eternity we will spend with our Lord. One day soon we will present ourselves at the marriage supper of the Lamb. I don't know about you, but I want to be prepared for that day.

THIRTEEN

The Need for a Healthy Lifestyle

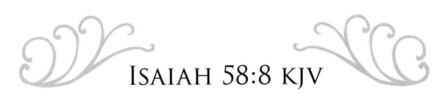

ISAIAH 58:8 KJV

Then shall thy light break forth as the morning,
and thine health shall spring forth speedily:
and thy righteousness shall go before thee;
the glory of the LORD shall be thy [rear guard NIV].

THE NEED FOR A HEALTHY LIFESTYLE

O ur primary purpose in fasting is to develop our spirits, not to lose weight. At the same time, though, fasting is a very healthy custom to adopt, and God works through this time of spiritual cleansing to cleanse our bodies, as well. While we bring the flesh into subjection to the Spirit of God and develop a deeper relationship with our heavenly Father, we get the side benefit of a more healthy body.

WHY OUR BODIES NEED BREAKS FROM FOOD

When you fast, your system has time to heal itself. More and more doctors are realizing how healthy it is to let the system have a time of restoration. It gives your internal organs time to recuperate. They work very hard most of the time. No wonder they occasionally rebel!

Our systems are cleansed to some degree while we sleep. But we don't always wake up in the morning ready to conquer the world. Sometimes more than eight hours is needed to flush all the toxins out of our systems.

Most of us abuse our digestive systems with the wrong kinds of food. Although God's people usually don't have the harmful habits of drinking, smoking, and doing drugs, many of them are killing themselves with food—with too much food and with the wrong kinds of food. This is not pleasing to God. We need to give our bodies, which are temples for the Holy Spirit, time for renewal, rest, and recuperation.

FASTING DOES A BODY GOOD

Many fear that fasting is harmful to your health. Nothing could be further from the truth. Moses fasted for forty days, but he didn't have to be carried down from the mountain at the end. In fact, when he came down, his face was glowing with the glory of the Lord.

> WE NEED TO GIVE OUR BODIES TIME FOR RENEWAL, REST, AND RECUPERATION.

If you follow God's leading in fasting, you will not grow unduly weak, and you will not ruin your health. Ladies, fasting will not destroy the beauty of your skin. If you fast enough, the glory of the Lord will shine forth from you, just as it did from the face of Moses. Believe the promise of God: *"Thine health shall spring forth speedily."*

Women who have problems with their menstrual cycles can be healed through fasting. God will perform miracles, and He will begin to realign their bodies. I have seen it happen.

I have known people with serious problems, some with cysts and growths the size of grapefruits. I have prayed with these individuals, and we've gone through fasting together. As we fast, God has actually dissolved the growth. Let me tell you, fasting is very powerful. God supernaturally restores people's health through it.

As we rest our organs, cleanse our systems, get control of our appetites, and develop more health-conscious lifestyles through fasting, we will feel the miraculous touch of God upon our lives. Fasting is the way to a healthy body, as well as a healthy spirit.

PART IV

THE NUTS AND BOLTS OF PRAYER AND FASTING—HOW TO DO IT AND DO IT WELL

INTRODUCTION
TO PART IV

A lot of people ask me, "How do you fast?" The truth is, fasting is something you just have to try in order to fully understand it. Much like learning to ride a bike or drive a car, fasting is best learned by experience. You just have to get out there and do it!

With all that being said, there are a few guidelines that can help ensure your fast is healthful and spiritually effective. In this closing section of *When Kings Pray and Fast*, we will examine steps to take before your fast and points to keep in mind during your fast so that your time of prayer and fasting will be glorifying to God and spiritually beneficial to you.

FOURTEEN

Fasting 101: Fundamentals of Fasting

DANIEL 9:3, 21–23

So I turned to the Lord God and pleaded with him in
prayer and petition, in fasting, and in sackcloth and ashes....
While I was still in prayer, Gabriel, the man I had seen in
the earlier vision, came to me in swift flight about the time
of the evening sacrifice. He instructed me and said to me,
"Daniel, I have now come to give you insight and understanding.
As soon as you began to pray, an answer was given, which
I have come to tell you, for you are highly esteemed."

FASTING 101:
FUNDAMENTALS
OF FASTING

S
o far, we've examined why many believers no longer practice prayer and fasting, as well as the biblical basis for
prayer and fasting and why we need to adopt this habit
in our lives. It is my prayer that you have a desire in your
spirit to pray and fast—a desire that you will realize by embarking
upon your own period of prayer and fasting.

Perhaps you still have many questions in your mind, such as:

- How long should I fast?
- Can I drink water or juice during a fast?
- Will I experience results from my fast right away?

We'll examine the answer to these and other questions in this
chapter.

TYPES OF FASTS

There are several different types of fasts. No mater what kind of
fast you choose, make sure you are immersed in prayer during your
time of fast—because fasting without prayer is just starvation.

WHEN KINGS PRAY AND FAST

NORMAL FAST

Also called the typical fast, this fast requires the faster to refrain from solid foods but allows him or her to drink liquids, which are usually limited to water and fruit juices.

Liquids serve the special purpose of helping to break down poisons in the body that are released during fasting. Lukewarm water with a little lemon or lime is most effective.

PARTIAL FAST

The partial fast is distinguished by the types of foods that may be eaten and how often those foods may be eaten. Usually people following a partial fast limit their food intake to fruits and vegetables and only eat during certain hours of the day.

For instance, a partial faster might choose to fast from the time he wakes up until 6 p.m. He may then eat at 6 p.m., but only those foods that are allowed by the fast (usually fruits and vegetables).

> **FASTING WITHOUT PRAYER IS STARVATION.**

Remember, you are not considered to be fasting while you sleep. Only count times when you are active during the day as "fasting hours."

A partial fast is a great training fast for those new to fasting. It is often the first type of fast people engage in before moving on to more extended periods of fasting.

COMPLETE FAST

Also called the absolute fast, this fast involves complete abstinence from both food and water. This is the type of fast Paul experienced after his conversion:

154

As he neared Damascus on his journey, suddenly a light from heaven flashed around him. He fell to the ground and heard a voice say to him, "Saul, Saul, why do you persecute me?" "Who are you, Lord?" Saul asked. "I am Jesus, whom you are persecuting," he replied. "Now get up and go into the city, and you will be told what you must do." The men traveling with Saul stood there speechless; they heard the sound but did not see anyone. Saul got up from the ground, but when he opened his eyes he could see nothing. So they led him by the hand into Damascus. For three days he was blind, and did not eat or drink anything. (Acts 9:3–9)

Many people avoid the complete fast for fear of hallucinations. This is an unfounded fear. In developing countries, the power of God has always manifested itself through periods of complete fasting. Remarkable breakthroughs that are seldom experienced in developed countries have been unleashed by complete fasts in developing nations.

> GOD WILL TAKE YOU OUT OF YOUR COMFORT ZONE, BUT HE WILL RENEW YOU.

So, do not be afraid to miss your meals. Wonderful things can happen through complete fasts. You will feel like you're in the wilderness during a complete fast, but remember: You cannot come into the promised land without going the way of the wilderness fast. God will take you out of your comfort zone during a complete fast, but He will renew and refresh you at the end.

Keep in mind that the complete fast, however, is a severe fast. It is considered an exceptional fast and should not be embarked upon unless an individual has been led to do so by the Lord.

Before beginning a complete fast, talk with your pastor and with your physician. They can help you take necessary steps to ensure that your fast is safe and effective.

DANIEL FAST

Also known as the twenty-one day fast, the Daniel fast is based on the fasting experiences of Daniel in the Old Testament:

> *At that time I, Daniel, mourned for three weeks. I ate no choice food; no meat or wine touched my lips; and I used no lotions at all until the three weeks were over.* (Daniel 10:2–3)

During this fast you eat no meat, no bread, no wine, no dessert. Basically, you avoid *"choice"* or *"pleasant"* (KJV) food. Your intake is limited to primarily fruits and vegetables, and these are usually eaten with little or no seasoning.

This type of fast is generally used to obtain revelation or guidance for a certain situation. In Daniel's case, answers to his prayers were unleashed as soon as he began fasting:

> *So I turned to the Lord God and pleaded with him in prayer and petition, in fasting, and in sackcloth and ashes....While I was speaking and praying, confessing my sin and the sin of my people Israel and making my request to the LORD my God for his holy hill—while I was still in prayer, Gabriel, the man I had seen in the earlier vision, came to me in swift flight about the time of the evening sacrifice. He instructed me and said to me, "Daniel, I have now come to give you insight and understanding. As soon as you began to pray, an answer was given, which I have come to tell you, for you are highly esteemed."* (Daniel 9:3, 20–23)

JUICE FAST

A juice fast can be used by those who are physically unable to do a complete fast. Like the partial fast, it may also be used as a training fast for those who wish to go onto more extended periods of fasting.

During a juice fast, never use concentrated juices or preprepared juices with high levels of sugar. Juices should be made from raw fruits and vegetables, not cooked ones. Such juices have live enzymes and nutrients, which are good for your body.

FREQUENCY OF FASTS

Every believer should have a personal consecration program that includes regular prayer and fasting. Ordinarily, a believer should fast at least one day per week. Periodically, at least once or twice a year, believers should also embark upon three-day fasts.

The three-day fast does something truly amazing for the faster. It is a glorious experience to receive Holy Communion after having completed a three-day fast. Occasionally after a three-day fast, a believer will feel led by the Lord to continue the fast into an extended fast.

> EVERY BELIEVER SHOULD REGULARLY PRACTICE PRAYER AND FASTING.

While your fasting should be a regular practice, it should not become so automatic that you take it "for granted" and lose sight of your purpose for fasting. Remember, *always* combine prayer with fasting; this will help you keep your eyes on the reasons for your fast.

WATER AND FASTING

More than 70 percent of the human body is water; even our bones are 30 percent water. Water helps with the elimination of toxins from our systems. It aids in digestion and proper blood circulation. It also helps us to maintain our energy levels, and it is crucial to the proper functioning of the nervous system, metabolism, muscle structure, and glands.

As you can see, for our bodies to function properly, water is essential. Without water, our health is impaired. The body can go a long time without food, but it can only go a few days without adequate liquids. Therefore, unless you are on a complete fast, make certain that you drink plenty of water.

Most people drink about eight glasses of water a day. My advice to you is to increase your water intake to twelve glasses a day three days before starting your fast. Then, during the fast, try to drink sixteen glasses. Do not wait until you are thirsty to drink water! Always keep yourself hydrated.

> THE BODY CAN GO A LONG TIME WITHOUT FOOD, BUT NOT WITHOUT WATER.

Water helps to flush the toxins that are released by fasting out of your system. Since you will not be getting the liquids normally contained in most foods, this is all the more reason to drink lots of water while you fast.

As a side note, do not be alarmed if your urine is very yellow during a fast. This just shows that your body is doing its job in getting rid of the toxins.

Be sure not to drink overly cold water during a fast. Your body processes warm water much more easily.

Many of us are addicted to sweets, and a fast is a good time to be set free from these cravings for sugar. Water will help you tremendously in getting over this craving. Putting a little lemon or lime in your water may help, as well.

In addition to keeping your body well hydrated, water plays another important role during seasons of fasting. I encourage people to take warm baths while they fast because baths are soothing and therapeutic. They will rejuvenate you and help keep you energized for the rest of your fast. For a detoxifying bath, add apple cider vinegar or Epsom salts to hot water. (NOTE: Always consult your physician before using Epsom salts.)

SLEEP AND FASTING

It's important during a fast to give your body the rest it needs. Do not physically overexert yourself during this time. A fast is not the time to start training for a marathon! Treat your body with care.

At the same time, spend as much time as possible in prayer. This may mean getting up in the middle of the night to pray sometimes if the Spirit prompts you to do so. Don't worry; the Spirit will give you the energy you need.

Let me honestly tell you that, at the height of your fast, you will not be able sleep like you normally do. Your spirit-man will be awake. Your eyes will be closed, but you will be seeing things in the Spirit while your body sleeps. I have had this happen to me many times, and it is a wonderful experience from the Lord.

A FAST IS NOT THE TIME TO START TRAINING FOR A MARATHON!

RESULTS OF FASTING

During a fast, the flesh gives way to the spirit-man, enabling the spirit-man to communicate better with God. Fasting secures God's results with God's blessings. As a result of fasting, you will experience:

- Improved health
- Answers to your prayers
- Spiritual direction and guidance
- Protection from the enemy
- Abundant spiritual blessing
- Peace and joy in the Spirit
- Emotional, physical, mental, spiritual, and relational restoration

Fasting will loose the bands of wickedness that might be binding your life. It will free you from heavy burdens and liberate you from oppression. After a fast, you will find yourself being more compassionate, more understanding, more in tune with God and His vision. As He reveals your own frailty to you through seasons of fasting, you will find yourself relying more and more upon Him and Him alone.

FIFTEEN

Fasting 201: Improving Your Fast

COLOSSIANS 3:23–24

Whatever you do, work at it with all your heart,
as working for the Lord, not for men, since you know
that you will receive an inheritance from the Lord as
a reward. It is the Lord Christ you are serving.

FASTING 201: IMPROVING YOUR FAST

Once you've got the basics of fasting down, it's time to move deeper. There's always more to learn—more ways to improve your prayer life and maximize the effectiveness of your fasting.

I do a forty-day fast every year, and I'll tell you something: Every day during that fast, I get progressively stronger in my spirit. And every year, my fast is better than the one from the year before. My prayer life continues to increase and grow. Praise God for the riches of His blessings!

Here are just a few lessons I have learned from my years of prayer and fasting. As you grow in your prayer life and develop your ability to fast, I am confident that the Lord will reveal new depths to you, as well. In turn, you can share these lessons with others.

DO NOT FEAR

The enemy doesn't like you, so settle that in your mind. He doesn't like me either.

He doesn't want us to succeed, especially when that success furthers the kingdom of God. He will try anything and everything to get us scared, to weaken us, to cause us to retreat. We're on his hit list, and he's out to get us.

But guess what? As much as he hates us, we hate him, too. Through Christ, we're going to make sure that his kingdom crumbles and that the kingdom of God stands strong!

YOU DON'T HAVE TO BE FEARFUL DURING A FAST.

When you go into periods of fasting, it might feel like you're fighting a battle—and you are! Satan knows that powerful results come from prayer and fasting, and he will fight hard to keep those results from coming to pass.

When you feel like you're in a battle, just remember to *"fear not"* (Deuteronomy 20:3 KJV). We have the Lord on our side, and so we have no need to fear!

> *When thou goest out to battle against thine enemies, and seest horses, and chariots, and a people more than thou, be not afraid of them: for the LORD thy God is with thee, which brought thee up out of the land of Egypt. And it shall be, when ye are come nigh unto the battle, that the priest shall approach and speak unto the people, and shall say unto them, Hear, O Israel, ye approach this day unto battle against your enemies: let not your hearts faint, fear not, and do not tremble, neither be ye terrified because of them; for the LORD your God is he that goeth with you, to fight for you against your enemies, to save you.*
>
> (Deuteronomy 20:1–4 KJV)

You don't have to be fearful during a fast. Just because you're not going to eat for a few days, don't get scared. Don't panic about not getting enough KFC this week or about missing out on pork chops one night. *"For the LORD your God is he that goeth with you, to fight for you against your enemies, to save you."* The Lord is with you!

CONCENTRATE ON THE WORD OF GOD

Once you have begun your fast, don't spend all your time in front of the television. For one thing, many advertisements are for food. Without thinking, you might get up, go to the refrigerator, and get something to eat. Don't set yourself up for failure like that!

The most important reason not to watch TV, however, is that it won't feed your soul. Neither will most magazines and other frivolous reading materials. Use this opportunity to get into the Word of God. Meditate on God's promises. Let your mind dwell on them. Claim them as your own.

> NOURISH YOUR SOUL WHILE YOU FAST; GET INTO THE WORD OF GOD.

For the word of God is living and active. Sharper than any double-edged sword, it penetrates even to dividing soul and spirit, joints and marrow; it judges the thoughts and attitudes of the heart. Nothing in all creation is hidden from God's sight. Everything is uncovered and laid bare before the eyes of him to whom we must give account. Therefore, since we have a great high priest who has gone through the heavens, Jesus the Son of God, let us hold firmly to the faith we profess.

(Hebrews 4:12–14)

The Word of God is powerful, so powerful that it can penetrate any obstacle, any circumstance, and any problem in life. It is more powerful than a two-edged sword, separating the spirit from the soul. Give yourself to the Word during your time of prayer and fasting.

DON'T NEGLECT PRAYER

The most important aspect of your fast is prayer. Remember, without prayer, fasting is nothing more than starvation. Here are a few tips for deepening your prayer life.

SHOW SATAN WHO'S BOSS

Prayer is a two-way conversation. Not only do we speak to God, but God speaks to us. When God is speaking, we shouldn't be thinking about last night's football game, drawing up our grocery list, or planning our next vacation. We need to be surrendered and completely listening to Him and Him alone.

> PRAYER IS A TWO-WAY CONVERSATION; WE NEED TO LISTEN TO GOD.

The enemy doesn't want us to communicate with the Father. Satan's goal is to get our minds on him and his activities, to distract us from the Lord. The most important thing you can do is just to keep your mind on God. Be aware of His presence with you. Be conscious of His working in your life. Pray His Word.

Remember, our principle purpose in prayer is not to wrestle with the enemy; it's to fellowship with the Lord. If you allow Satan to dominate your prayer time, he will. He'll come up with all kinds of distractions to turn your eyes away from heaven. Don't waste your time on him! Satan has no right to interrupt our intimate time of fellowship with God. Cast him out. Send him on his way. Don't yield your valuable time to the enemy.

FASTING 201: IMPROVING YOUR FAST

Submit yourselves, then, to God. Resist the devil, and he will flee from you. (James 4:7)

Do not give the devil a foothold. (Ephesians 4:27)

Don't pray for the devil to go; command him to go! Ask God for wisdom and authority on how to deal with the enemy, and then, without wasting any more precious time, put him to flight. Use the authority God has given you, and tell the enemy to leave. Let him know that he has no right to disturb you while you are communing with the Father.

Satan knows that he has no right to interrupt the activities of my home. He knows that the members of my family are covered by the blood of Jesus. He knows that he doesn't belong in our house. He knows to whom we belong, and he has no right to touch us. I am not afraid of him, and he knows it.

> USE THE AUTHORITY GOD HAS GIVEN YOU AND TELL SATAN TO LEAVE.

SENSE THE PRESENCE OF GOD

Many people do not get their prayers answered because they cannot sense the Lord's presence. These people cannot visualize Him, so how could they talk intimately with Him? How can you converse with God effectively if you cannot sense His presence?

When most people think about Jesus, they picture Him on the cross in agony. They weep for Him. They plead for mercy for Him. They ask the Father to be compassionate to Jesus. Because of this, they can't get any further in their prayers. How can Jesus help us if He is in agony Himself?

We must know that Jesus hung on the cross for a short space of time. He was in the grave for a short space of time. And then He overcame death! He is alive, not on the cross! See Him triumphant. See Him reigning.

See Jesus. Look into His face. Talk to Him. Tell Him your troubles. Confide in Him. Bare your soul before Him.

When you think of Jesus, don't envision a painting somebody did of Him. No human has ever, or will ever, capture the glory of the Son of God with a paintbrush!

Look to the Jesus of the Bible, not the Jesus of popular myth. He is the King of Glory, not just another prophet. He is Lord of All, not just a good teacher. See the living God, and receive from His hand.

PRAY TO PRAISE

Many people have the "gimmes." They only fast when they want to get something material. They go to God with their wish lists and hope fasting will boost their chances of getting everything they want.

> WE FAST TO GLORIFY GOD, NOT TO GET THINGS.

Don't trivialize fasting. We do not fast just to receive things or to get answers to specific prayers. We fast for the sake of our spiritual position with God. We fast to glorify Him. We fast to grow closer to our Father.

When you fast, seek to understand and experience the love of God; other things will come as a result. *"But seek first his kingdom and his righteousness, and all these things will be given to you as well"* (Matthew 6:33).

Begin your prayers by acknowledging God's love and by expressing your love for Him. Worship Him. Adore Him. Glorify Him. Work toward a deeper expression of your mutual love.

FASTING 201: IMPROVING YOUR FAST

TAKE TIME TO CONFESS

Acknowledge your failings and shortcomings in prayer before the Lord. Early in your prayer time, confess your sins to the Father and allow Him to cleanse your heart, to wash you clean. Then your heart will be open to hearing all the Father has to share with you.

Most people have so many things standing between them and God that they need several days just to clear the air and prepare for good communication. Fasting is not just for the purpose of resolving specific problems. It has the purpose of renewing and strengthening your relationship with God, so that your everyday prayers can be more effective.

Pray as David did:

Search me, O God, and know my heart; test me and know my anxious thoughts. See if there is any offensive way in me, and lead me in the way everlasting. (Psalms 139:23–24)

If you fast, yet you have something in your heart against your neighbor—a grudge, unforgivingness, bitterness, strife, envy—don't expect to get miracles from God. Any of those things will bring you into bondage if they are allowed to rule in your heart. Use your time in prayer and fasting to bring those things to light so that God can deal with them.

INTERCEDE FOR OTHERS

Before you pray for your own needs, intercede for others. Pray the heart of God. You won't lose anything by doing this. God is concerned about your most insignificant need, but He is also concerned that you be like the One who laid everything down to serve others. When you have prayed for others, the Father will stretch out His hand to you and invite you to receive all that you are personally lacking.

Intercede for the leaders of your nation. Intercede for community leaders. And intercede for your spiritual leaders. It is easy to criticize our leaders, but few are willing to give the time and effort necessary to intercede in prayer for those in authority. If we believe that God is powerful, we should be willing to ask for His help in every matter, both public and private. If we believe the old saying, "Prayer changes things," then let's put it to work.

We are admonished by Jesus Himself to pray for more laborers for the spiritual harvest. If we should pray for them to go into the field, surely we can uphold them during their labors there. They are human, and they will make mistakes, but we are not called to judge them. God is the judge. We are called to uphold God's servants in prayer.

Present Your Own Needs

When you have taken all these steps, it is time to present your own needs before the Lord—and you may do so with great boldness!

Do not be anxious about anything, but in everything, by prayer and petition, with thanksgiving, present your requests to God. And the peace of God, which transcends all understanding, will guard your hearts and your minds in Christ Jesus.

(Philippians 4:6–7)

God shows His interest in your need by His concern with your *"daily bread"* (Matthew 6:11). He wants to supply for you personally. Don't be hesitant to take your petitions before Him. Do it boldly. God wants to help you.

Hold Steady at the Start

Be firm during the first three days of your fast. They are the most difficult because your body experiences withdrawal symptoms, similar to how a drug addict goes through withdrawal when trying to stop drugs. Your symptoms won't be this severe, but your body will start to react. Your body is accustomed to having food, and it doesn't like being denied.

It is during the first three days that many people quit. If you have a genuine burden for the lost, if you want to see drug addicts delivered, if you want to see our society changed by God's power, then you will continue.

Be firm. When those first days have passed, it will become easier.

> DON'T DRAW ATTENTION TO THE FACT THAT YOU'RE FASTING.

LOOK FRESH

When you fast, don't go out of your way to look fatigued. Don't draw attention to the fact that you are fasting. Don't try to get everyone's sympathy by complaining about how hungry you are.

Remember what Jesus said?

When you fast, do not look somber as the hypocrites do, for they disfigure their faces to show men they are fasting. I tell you the truth, they have received their reward in full. But when you fast, put oil on your head and wash your face, so that it will not be obvious to men that you are fasting, but only to your Father, who is unseen; and your Father, who sees what is done in secret, will reward you. (Matthew 6:16–18)

There are some people who don't shower when they fast. They don't comb their hair or brush their teeth. This is not something I suggest doing. Your goal is not supposed to be to draw people's attention to the fact that you're fasting. So don't do it!

BE AWARE OF SPECIAL NEEDS

Some people need to get away from everyone while they are fasting because the normal activities of the household might disturb their concentration. You don't need to go far or spend a lot of money on a hotel room. Most churches have rooms that are not in use and could be made available for prayer.

Sometimes we just need to get away from all the rush and go to a private place. We need to set ourselves apart from everyday activities. My wife encourages me whenever I feel this need. She understands and supports me.

Some people need to take time off from work to seek the face of God. If we can take time off for vacations, for hunting season, or just to work around the house for a few days, why not do it for the welfare of our souls?

If you are married, consider sleeping apart from your spouse while you are fasting. Deny the flesh.

> *Defraud ye not one the other, **except it be with consent for a time, that ye may give yourselves to fasting and prayer;** and come together again, that Satan tempt you not for your incontinency.* (1 Corinthians 7:5 KJV, emphasis added)

Agree with your spouse for a period of abstinence from your physical relationship for the purpose of seeking God. This will not hurt your relationship. It will strengthen it.

END WISELY

When your fast has ended and you begin to eat normally again, use wisdom. Some people do really crazy things. During their fast, they save back all the food they would have eaten. After they finish the fast, they gorge themselves, destroying all the spiritual and physical benefits they would have derived from the fast.

Begin to eat slowly, not all at once. And use the opportunity to develop better, healthier eating habits. Now that you have the flesh under control, this will be easier to do.

SIXTEEN

Stop Making Excuses!

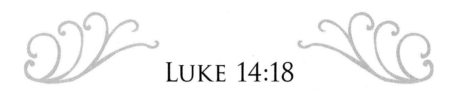

LUKE 14:18

But they all alike began to make excuses.

STOP MAKING EXCUSES!

J ust like those who were invited to the feast in the parable Jesus told in Luke 14, everyone seems to have an excuse for not fasting. Here are just a few of the most common— and why they don't fly.

YOUNG PEOPLE AND FASTING

Some young people think they are "too young" to fast. When our daughter Anna was very young, we allowed her to miss a meal occasionally, even though she was too young to understand well what she was doing. She couldn't fully understand the needs of the local church. She couldn't fully understand the problems of the ministry. Nevertheless, by permitting her to fast, we knew that we were equipping her early to know how to seek the face of God.

If all of us had begun to pray and fast at a younger age, many of us would not have gotten into so many problems in adolescence and young adulthood. I thank God for parents who encouraged me in prayer and fasting. They wanted more than anything else to see me in the will of God for my life.

177

Young people, don't let anyone tell you that fasting is not from God or is no longer important. Don't let anyone tell you that you don't need to fast. Take authority over your appetites, and don't let your belly run your life. Submit yourself to God so that you can get your every prayer answered.

> STAND ON THE WORDS OF JESUS, AND DON'T LET ANYONE DISCOURAGE YOU.

Remember, when the disciples asked, "Why couldn't we do it? What is the secret?" Jesus answered them, "This kind goes not out but by prayer and fasting." (See Matthew 17:19–21 KJV.)

Stand on the words of Jesus, and don't let anyone discourage you from doing His will for your life. As young people, you have a whole lifetime ahead of you. Start seizing the opportunities God has given you early on. Get serious with God, and His blessing will be upon you.

Parents, don't deny your children and young people the opportunity to seek the face of God in prayer and fasting if and when they desire to do so.

THE ELDERLY AND FASTING

On the other end of the spectrum, some elderly people think they are "too old" to fast. If you are a diabetic, perhaps you have a legitimate reason not to fast—but only until you get set free from your sickness. I have known many people who received healing from various diseases while they were fasting. Don't limit God.

For those elderly persons who are well, there is no excuse. Anna the prophetess should be an example to every elderly person concerning fasting.

Stop Making Excuses!

*There was also a prophetess, Anna, the daughter of Phanuel, of the tribe of Asher. **She was very old;** she had lived with her husband seven years after her marriage, and then was a widow until she was eighty-four. She never left the temple but worshiped night and day, fasting and praying. Coming up to them at that very moment, she gave thanks to God and spoke about the child to all who were looking forward to the redemption of Jerusalem.*

(Luke 2:36–38, emphasis added)

Anna fasted regularly even though she was *"very old."* Fasting and prayer developed in her a sensitivity to the Spirit of God, so that, when almost everyone failed to recognize the child Jesus as being different from other children his age, Anna was miraculously drawn to Him and saw Him for who He was.

Elderly people don't want to fast for the same reason the rest of us don't want to fast. We have accustomed our stomachs to certain foods at certain times of the day, and we don't like to feel hungry. We enjoy eating.

I would say to the elderly among us that God isn't finished with you yet. You have a very great responsibility before God to share your knowledge of Him with the upcoming generations. Be the example you should be in prayer and fasting.

Men and Fasting

Some men don't fast because they believe they must spend their free time with their families. However, a good father and true leader of a household is one who can hear the voice of God and know God's will for his family.

Some men never fast because they have to work, and they cannot get alone with God for long periods. If you must work, that doesn't mean that you cannot fast. Many of God's people who have

179

to work fast anyway. Just ask the Lord to help you keep your mind on Him. When lunchtime comes, don't hang around to see what the others will eat. Get alone, perhaps in your car or in some other private place. Get your Bible, and concentrate on the mind of the Lord. But take time out to fast.

Men, we have a great responsibility. Because we know that we are living in the last days and that the coming of the Lord is growing nearer, we should be compelled to pray and fast even more. Those who are not conscious of the lateness of the hour never fast.

> *Jesus answered, "How can the guests of the bridegroom fast while he is with them? They cannot, so long as they have him with them. But the time will come when the bridegroom will be taken from them, and on that day **they will fast**."*
>
> (Mark 2:19–20, emphasis added)

Jesus said that we should fast when the bridegroom was taken away. Fasting will continue, then, until His return. Don't stop now. There is too much to be accomplished in the kingdom of God.

After more than thirty-nine years in the ministry, God is dealing with me now more than ever about fasting. This is not a time to relax and allow ourselves to be ruled by the flesh. We must hone our spiritual instincts and be ready to do spiritual warfare in these last days. Don't let the women do all the fasting. If we do, they will get all the blessings.

WOMEN AND FASTING

In general, women fast more than men, but even women have their excuses for not fasting. The two most predominant excuses women use are their need to prepare food for the whole family and their need to maintain good appearances. Neither of these should be an excuse not to fast when the Lord leads you to do so.

Stop Making Excuses!

If you need to prepare food for the rest of the family, you can do that and still continue your fast. It just demands a little more willpower on your part not to sample dinner while you're cooking it. When your husband and your children eat, read your Bible and spend time in prayer. Meditate on the goodness of God. You can serve others while abstaining yourself.

As for appearance, it is a lie of Satan that fasting destroys your appearance. My mother is still strong and looks fresh and beautiful—because of her life of fasting and prayer.

> WE NEED TO STOP BELIEVING SATAN'S LIES.

Women, stop believing Satan's lies.

THE LAMEST EXCUSES

Feeling that you are too old or too young or too sick or too busy are poor excuses for not fasting. Here are some examples of lame excuses for not fasting.

- Some actually think they are going to die if they fast. "Why take the chance?" they ask.

- Some feel like they are having some type of reaction, that they can't breathe. "It's too hard for me," they say. And they discontinue their fast.

- Some intend to fast—next year. They always have good intentions, but they're for the future, not for today.

- Some actually fast—breakfast, lunch, and dinner. Then they eat like pigs and fall into the bed to "sleep it off."

- Some people feel that it is enough to abstain from food from bedtime to breakfast.

- Some people feel they cannot function without meat in their stomachs.

- Some people fast for wrong motives. If you want to serve God, serve Him with a pure motive. If you want to deny the flesh, then do it. Stop making excuses.

- Some people profess to fast just so they can please others. The truth is that, on the way home, they stop at McDonald's and eat heartily. They think they are fooling someone. But they can't fool God. Fasting is not for the pleasure of other people; fasting is done unto God. This is a serious matter. Why play games with God? If you cannot be sincere in a fast, God won't be able to trust you with His blessings.

- Some don't fast because they fear they will be "misunderstood," and they don't want to be criticized. While it's true that some people may be critical of you and say that you are "anti-social," it's worth it to walk in the power and anointing of God. When these same people have a need, they will know who to call on. When effective prayers must be prayed, they will remember your dedication to God. Don't let what other people think or say hinder you. Obey God.

NO EXCUSE

Right now, today, you must face the thing that has kept you from fasting and conquer it once and for all.

If gluttony has kept you from God's best, He is ready to deliver you from that sin. If food has been controlling you, cast it down from its throne today and let Christ reign and be the Lord of your life. If your belly has been your god, make Jehovah, God of our fathers, your God today.

If you have a medical problem that prevents you from fasting, God is able to heal you. If His will is for His people to fast, and you are one of His children, His will is that you fast. And if you cannot fast because of a medical problem, He wants to remove that obstacle so that you can have total victory in your life. Be healed in the name of Jesus Christ today.

If God is leading you to fast, then fast. Lay aside every excuse, conquer the flesh, and just do it.

SEVENTEEN

Prepare Yourself for Prayer and Fasting

1 Corinthians 9:27 KJV

But I keep under my body, and bring it into subjection:
lest that by any means, when I have preached
to others, I myself should be a castaway.

PREPARE YOURSELF FOR PRAYER AND FASTING

Your declaration, your commitment to prayer and fasting, is more for yourself than it is for others. When I declare that I am going to fast, I am taking the first step toward preparing myself. I know that what I am about to do may be difficult for my flesh, and so I put every part of my being on alert, letting my body know what I intend to do, what is about to come.

I prepare myself. My mind is made up, my emotions are under control, and my body is ready to obey. I know exactly what I am about to do: pray, fast, and seek the face of God.

Once I have made that declaration, the responsibility to carry through on my commitment is mine. It will not be easy; I must prepare myself to obey. I must discipline myself and make myself fast. I must say to myself, "I will bring my spirit, my body, my emotions, and my mind all under subjection to the Word of God by giving myself to prayer and fasting." (See 1 Corinthians 9:27 KJV.)

Get yourself ready to do something great. God does not waste a prepared vessel. He has much work to be done. He is looking for those who are ready to be placed into positions of authority.

FASTING IS LIKE...

Fasting provides incredible results. But incredible results always require considerable preparation. I like to liken fasting to a race, to a hike, and to a battle. In each case, your preparation is your key to success. Let me explain.

...A RACE

Before an athlete enters a race, he must prepare for it. Can you imagine showing up for a race without training for it first? Can you imagine participating in a 5K if you hadn't run an inch in the past five years?

> FASTING IS LIKE A RACE, A HIKE, AND A BATTLE— THEY ALL TAKE PREPARATION.

It's just as absurd to enter into prayer and fasting without preparation. Your ultimate goal is to run a successful race, right? To cross the finish line? To run your best? To win? If so, then you need to prepare, just as an athlete has to prepare for a race.

How do you prepare yourself? How do you train for fasting? You start small and build up. Begin to eliminate certain things that are not essential in your diet, for instance, and work from there.

So, if somebody tells you you can't fast for a day or two or three—or twenty-one, or thirty, or forty—it's a lie. There are many people who have done it many times, and you can do it to. You just have to work up to it.

It won't happen overnight. Just like successfully running a race, it will take training. But you can do it.

...A HIKE

Fasting is also like a hike. How? Well, when you find someone who's going on hike, they have gear. Right? They don't traipse into the woods with no food, no compass, no shelter. They don't venture out with flip-flops on their feet. They've prepared themselves first. They have the proper gear and are ready for what lies ahead.

The same principle holds true for fasting. We must prepare ourselves first. Equip yourself before starting a fast. Get ready for the days ahead. Don't venture out unprepared.

Fasting is like a hike in another way, as well. The ultimate desire of a hiker is to explore, and the same desire guides a person who is fasting. Fasting helps you explore—spiritually, physically, mentally, and emotionally. You'll find many things that most people don't even know exist.

...A BATTLE

Finally, fasting is like a battle. Fasting doesn't come easy, and it's a struggle, a battle, at times. Your spirit has to fight because every part of your flesh, your mind, and your emotions will war against the fast.

Like a soldier going into battle, you must prepare yourself for the fight ahead. And you must prepare yourself for victory. A soldier doesn't go into a battle planning to lose or to be killed, does he? No! He goes in planning to be victorious and to come out alive. Your approach to fasting must be the same. You *will* come out victorious; plan on it.

PHYSICAL PREPARATION

We've already established that your body will want to rebel against fasting. Here are a few things you can do to prepare yourself physically for the rigors of fasting.

BEFORE YOU FAST

Before you even start your fast, make sure you're drinking plenty of water. You need to keep yourself hydrated during a fast, so start early. Increase your water intake in the days leading up to your fast.

Start cutting back on the number of times you eat each day. If you usually eat four times a day, cut back to three. If you eat three times a day, cut back to two. This will prepare your body for the fast ahead.

GIVE YOUR BODY PEP TALKS DURING YOUR FAST.

If you have a physical ailment, notify your doctor about your upcoming fast and ask for his or her involvement in your decision. Your doctor can give you advice on how to physically prepare for the fast ahead.

As a side note, many people have medications that can't be taken on an empty stomach. My personal advice for those who take medications like this is to continue the medicine and just eat a few fruits or vegetables if necessary.

If you drink coffee regularly, start cutting back. You shouldn't consume caffeine while you're fasting, so you need to prepare now. If you stop drinking coffee cold turkey whenever you start your fast, you may get headaches.

WHILE YOU FAST

When you start your fast, your body is going to complain. It's going to put up a fight, and it's going to rebel. What you need to do is give your body pep talks. Tell your stomach, "You are not going to die, because I decided I'm not dying yet, so hang in there." Talk to your belly, show it who's boss, and your fast will be easier.

You may occasionally experience headaches while you're fasting. These headaches are in response to the toxins in your body—toxins from the foods you've eaten that are then released by the fast. Water will help flush these toxins out of your system and alleviate your headaches, so drink plenty of it.

During your fast, don't do anything strenuous. Now is not the time to go jogging, lift weights, or play a long game of basketball. Don't wear your body out when it's fasting. You've replaced physical exercise with spiritual exercise anyway. Focus on your spiritual workout.

ENDING YOUR FAST

Preparing for the end of your fast is just as important as preparing for the fast itself. Many people go overboard after a fast. Because they haven't eaten in so long, they make up for it in the days following their fast. These people end up undoing all the good things brought about by their fasts. Sometimes they actually end up worse off than they were before their fast.

End your fast in fellowship with God. Say a prayer of thanksgiving to Him, praising Him for bringing you through the fast and nourishing you spiritually through it. Have a worship service with fellow believers, and maybe even share in Holy Communion. End your fast in a spirit of praise and celebration.

In the physical realm, come out of your fast gradually. For an extended fast, use the following guidelines:

Day 1—Juice only.

Day 2—Add fruit.

Day 3—Add soup.

Day 4—Add salads.

Day 5—Add whole grain breads, pastas, etc.

Day 6—Add fish or chicken. (Save beef for after your body has adjusted.)

Remember to watch the quantity of food you consume as you come out of a fast. It's tempting to overeat, but be moderate in your eating. Rest as much as possible, and continue in a spirit of prayer for ultimate benefits from your fast.

EIGHTEEN

Make a Commitment to Commitment to Prayer and Fasting

PROVERBS 1:23 KJV

Behold, I will pour out my
spirit unto you, I will make known
my words unto you.

MAKE A COMMITMENT
TO PRAYER AND FASTING

To be successful in prayer and fasting, it is crucial to make a commitment to it and then follow through. You must make a commitment of time and effort to prayer and fasting or else you will never reap the benefits. This commitment to fast is then finalized by making a proclamation, by making your intentions known.

THE POWER OF PROCLAIMING

The word *preach* comes from the Greek word *kerusso*. It means "to proclaim, to make known or declare." When Jesus spoke to those gathered in the synagogue at Nazareth, He said that the Spirit of the Lord was upon Him to proclaim, to make known, and to declare the gospel to the poor.

He went to Nazareth, where he had been brought up, and on the Sabbath day he went into the synagogue, as was his custom. And he stood up to read. The scroll of the prophet Isaiah was handed to him. Unrolling it, he found the place where it is written: "The Spirit of the Lord is on me, because he has anointed me to preach good news to the poor. He has sent me to proclaim freedom for the prisoners and recovery of sight for the blind, to release

195

the oppressed, to proclaim the year of the Lord's favor." Then he
rolled up the scroll, gave it back to the attendant and sat down.
The eyes of everyone in the synagogue were fastened on him, and
he began by saying to them, "Today this scripture is fulfilled in
your hearing."   (Luke 4:16–21)

The Spirit of the Lord was upon Him to proclaim, to make known, and to declare deliverance to the captives. The Lord was upon Him to proclaim, to make known, and to declare the acceptable year of the Lord. Jesus knew the importance of proclaiming.

Proclamation, or making something known, is very important. The Scriptures say,

For it is with your heart that you believe and are justified, and it
is with your mouth that you confess and are saved.
                                                  (Romans 10:10)

EVERY BELIEVER
IS A PREACHER,
ONE WHO
PROCLAIMS.

We confess Jesus Christ as Lord and are saved. In this sense, every believer is a preacher, one who proclaims. When we confess Jesus as Lord, we are preaching and proclaiming His lordship.

To be successful in the believer's life, we must proclaim to ourselves first and foremost. We must speak God's Word to ourselves. We must remind ourselves of His promises and of the commitments we have made to Him.

Once is not enough. Every day we need to remind ourselves of the grace of God in our lives. We need to proclaim it, to make it known. We must declare God's favor toward ourselves frequently. We must daily preach the gospel to our own hearts.

Proclaiming Your Fast

When I have declared my faith to others, they are justified in expecting me to live up to my confession, or profession, of faith. When they look at me, they may do so based on the declaration I have made. I am bound by my confession, my proclamation. When I tell someone that I am saved, they expect to see new life in me. When I say that I love the Lord, people are justified in expecting to see that declaration lived out in my words and actions.

Because proclaiming is so powerful, we must proclaim our fasts if we want to succeed. We must declare it—to ourselves and to others.

When you proclaim a fast, the devil might try to tell you that you are a hypocrite, trying to draw attention to yourself. The Bible does say, *"When you give to the needy, do not let your left hand know what your right hand is doing"* (Matthew 6:3). But this just means that we are not to boast about what we are doing. What we do is to be done unto God, not unto men. This does not, however, prevent us from declaring what we are about to do.

> WE MUST PROCLAIM OUR FASTS IF WE WANT TO SUCCEED.

Some people really put on a show when they fast. They try to look absolutely miserable. They don't bathe. They keep looking in the mirror to see how their condition is, as if they were about to die at any minute. "Do I look pale to you?" they ask.

This is not the kind of declaration I am speaking of. The confessions we make are not for vainglory. They are to get ourselves and others around us ready for what we are about to do. We make a public commitment so that we can't easily change our minds for every flimsy excuse. Personally, I have found that declaring my fasts eliminates much of the struggle I might otherwise have in obeying God.

DON'T JUST SAY IT: BELIEVE IT

In order to make a declaration to fast, you must first be convinced that you should do it. If your heart and will are not set on it, your declaration will be just empty words. We must believe what we declare.

Toward the end of every year, people begin making their New Year's resolutions. Some decide to lose some weight. Others commit to stop smoking or to break some other bad habit. The great majority keep these well-intentioned resolutions for only a few days.

Why? Usually it's because they didn't believe what they were resolving in the first place. They weren't serious and didn't make a commitment from the heart. Caught up in the emotion of the passing of another year, they resolved. But their resolve wasn't very effective because their hearts weren't behind it. Our proclamations, our commitments to fast, must be different from this wavering human resolve. Our confessions must be bolstered and supported by the Holy Spirit.

Most believers have, at one time or another, made a commitment to fast "after Thanksgiving." But after Thanksgiving, someone invites them to KFC and offers them some of those large biscuits. Then Christmas comes. Then New Year's. Then birthdays. Then the Fourth of July. And on and on—it never ends. There are enough special days in the year to keep us breaking our resolve forever.

With many people, because there is not a firm commitment to fasting in the first place, any excuse to avoid it will do. This is why it is necessary to make a proclamation concerning fasting and to make that proclamation from a determined heart. You must personally make a statement, to yourself and others, that you intend to fast for a certain period of time. Once made, you must keep your commitment, for making a confession places you in a position of responsibility before God and before man.

COMMITMENT PHOBIA

Many people are fearful of commitment. They know it costs something, and they are afraid that they may not be able to fulfill their part. They say they would rather not promise than have to break that promise later. When you make excuses like this, you actually *are* making a commitment—to failure and to mediocrity.

When I invite people to come to our services, some answer, "Pastor, I don't want to promise you that I will come, because something might happen so that I can't make it. I will try to make it—if I can. But please don't count on me."

> WE MUST BELIEVE WHAT WE SAY OR ELSE IT'S JUST EMPTY WORDS.

I doubt if that type of person will ever fully understand the kingdom of God. How can you place authority or trust in people who are afraid to make any commitment? You can't! James said that a person like this is a *"double-minded man, unstable in all he does"* (James 1:8).

Make up your mind. If you want to be part of God's kingdom, then make a commitment to do it. If you want to receive the blessings of a local faith community, then make a commitment to be an active part of that church. If you want to hear God's voice, then make a commitment to pray and fast.

In his epistle, James also wrote,

WHEN KINGS PRAY AND FAST

When he asks, he must believe and not doubt, because he who doubts is like a wave of the sea, blown and tossed by the wind. That man should not think he will receive anything from the Lord. (James 1:6–7)

This is strong language: *"That man should not think he will receive anything from the Lord."* Did you catch that? The man who doubts should not expect to receive *anything*. Anything! God cannot trust a wavering person. Such a person is not reliable. His line is always, "Well, I am not going to tell you that I will do this. I would like to, but perhaps I can't. And I wouldn't want to disappoint you." What a lame excuse! And yet so many people use it!

> IT IS BETTER TO COMMIT AND FAIL THAN NEVER TO COMMIT AT ALL.

It is better to commit and have to break a commitment and suffer the consequences than never to make a commitment of any kind. Those who never make a commitment to fast will never end up fasting.

This half-hearted approach to everything seems acceptable in our society today: No commitment in marriage, no commitment on the job, no commitment among friends. If you commit yourself, you might have to do something whether you want to or not. So why take the chance?

No wonder few people fast! It demands too much of them!

I understand why many believers have so little joy. They are not willing to make a full commitment to Christ. They are trying to live on the fence—with one foot in the kingdom and the other in the flesh. This simply won't work. People who live like that are the most miserable people alive.

Make a Commitment to Prayer and Fasting

If you make a commitment to fast and something legitimate prevents you from keeping it, don't worry. Just make a new commitment and keep it this time around. The key is to make a commitment.

You cannot expect results from your faith if you are unwilling to commit to Him who is the object of your faith. You cannot expect to see the Word of God fulfilled in your life if you are unwilling to commit to that Word. And you cannot expect to see the results of prayer and fasting if you are unwilling to commit to prayer and fasting. Please, make a commitment. It's worth it. Believe me.

Corporate and Personal Commitments

It is very biblical for a pastor or other leader to call for an entire congregation to fast. Some people rebel and say, "I don't fast just because the pastor says I should; I'll fast when the Lord tells me to fast. God can speak to me personally." These people almost never fast. If they are unwilling to join a public fast, they will most likely not fast on their own.

If a fast is not called by a spiritual leader, it becomes a very personal thing—something between you and God. Give Him the opportunity to speak to you. God doesn't tell some people to fast because they don't want to hear it. Their ears are stopped, and their minds are made up. God doesn't waste words; He won't spend them on people who won't listen. If you are open, though, He will speak to you.

If many months go by and you haven't been led to fast, get concerned. That is not normal. The disciples fasted regularly. So did many congregations during the Reformation. Read God's Word until you become convinced of your need to fast. Then make your commitment.

You will be very hesitant to make a commitment to prayer and fasting if you doubt your ability to fulfill such a commitment. Those who are unsure can start out with shorter periods of fasting. There is no biblical rule about how long you must fast. It is okay to begin on a smaller scale and work your way up as you feel able.

Perhaps you have been feeling a little weak physically and are not sure if you are able to complete a fast. Perhaps you are not feeling the best because of a recent bout of the flu or because of extra hours put in at work or for some other reason. There is no better way to improve your health and receive divine healing than fasting.

> MAKE A COMMITMENT TO FAST UNTIL THE LORD TELLS YOU TO STOP FASTING.

If you are unsure of the timing of your fast—when you should begin and how long you should fast—you may hesitate to make a commitment. But it isn't always necessary to know how long you will fast before you begin. If the Lord leads you to begin a fast and doesn't tell you how long to go, trust Him to tell you when it is time to quit. Make a commitment to fast until the Lord tells you to stop fasting.

If you feel burdened to fast and don't know when to begin, know that the same God who urges you to fast can tell you exactly when to do it. Just make the commitment; He will see you through it.

I congratulate those of you who have fasted in the past and those of you who have been challenged by this book and are about to embark on a journey into the realm of fasting and prayer and seeking the face of God. You will experience great breakthroughs in the Spirit. You are about to get control over your appetites once and for all. You are about to hear from God in a new and living way. You are about to have your faith increased.

Conclusion

CONCLUSION

There are many biblical examples of kings throughout the ages who have led their nations and people in periods of fasting to see the hand of God move on their behalf. During his reign, King Jehoshaphat of Judah loved the Lord and sought to honor Him by turning the hearts of the people to the Lord and teaching them God's ways. In 2 Chronicles, we learn that when Jehoshaphat was confronted by a vast army of Moabites and Ammonites, he called a fast and led the nation in prayer:

And Jehoshaphat feared, and set himself to seek the LORD, and proclaimed a fast throughout all Judah. And Judah gathered themselves together, to ask help of the LORD: even out of all the cities of Judah they came to seek the LORD. And Jehoshaphat stood in the congregation of Judah and Jerusalem, in the house of the LORD, before the new court, and said, O LORD God of our fathers, art not thou God in heaven? And rulest not thou over all the kingdoms of the heathen? And in thine hand is there not power and might, so that none is able to withstand thee? Art not thou our God, who didst drive out the inhabitants of this land before thy people Israel, and gavest it to the seed of Abraham thy friend for ever? And they dwelt therein, and have built thee a sanctuary therein for thy name, saying, If, when evil cometh upon us, as the sword, judgment, or pestilence, or famine, we stand before this house, and in thy presence, (for thy name is in this house,) and cry unto thee in our affliction, then thou wilt hear and help. (2 Chronicles 20:3–9 KJV)

Jahaziel, one of David's mighty warriors, responded with prophecy to Jehoshaphat's prayer:

Hearken ye, all Judah, and ye inhabitants of Jerusalem, and thou king Jehoshaphat, thus saith the LORD unto you, Be not afraid nor dismayed by reason of this great multitude; for the battle is not yours, but God's. Tomorrow go ye down against them: behold, they come up by the cliff of Ziz; and ye shall find them at the end of the brook, before the wilderness of Jeruel. Ye shall not need to fight in this battle: set yourselves, stand ye still, and see the salvation of the LORD with you, O Judah and Jerusalem: fear not, nor be dismayed; tomorrow go out against them: for the LORD will be with you. (2 Chronicles 20:15–17 KJV)

God delivered Jehoshaphat and his nation from the hands of their enemies because they came together in prayer and acknowledged Him as the God of their fathers, who rules over all kingdoms.

Ezra, another biblical leader, called the returning Jews to fast and pray for their return from exile:

There, by the Ahava Canal, I proclaimed a fast, so that we might humble ourselves before our God and ask him for a safe journey for us and our children, with all our possessions. I was ashamed to ask the king for soldiers and horsemen to protect us from enemies on the road, because we had told the king, "The gracious hand of our God is on everyone who looks to him, but his great anger is against all who forsake him." So we fasted and petitioned our God about this, and he answered our prayer. (Ezra 8:21–23)

God is with those who pray and fast, submitting their wills to His and trusting in Him to deliver them from whatever they are going through.

CONCLUSION

There are many other examples of kings and leaders who led their people to pray and fast when their kingdoms or nations were at stake. But what matters most is whether you are going to be an example in your day and in your area of a king who prays and fasts.

We are joint heirs with Christ and thus have His kingly power and authority. As kings with Christ, we must encourage those around us to unite in prayer and fasting, claiming for our own the power that God has made available to us. We are God's kingly ambassadors on earth, and we must bring those around us to the spiritual feast God has prepared for His children.

With the power that comes through regular prayer and fasting, we can see our lost loved ones come into the fold. We can see those with terminal illnesses healed and completely renewed. We can see families restored, churches revived, and nations rebuilt.

We have the answer for the downtrodden and the homeless. We have the answer for unwed mothers struggling to provide for their children. We have the answer for those trapped on welfare; for those who are hungry, lost, cold, oppressed, sick, weary, and searching.

A Christianity that doesn't reach out beyond the four walls of the church is ineffective. It is not Christianity at all. True Christianity shows God's love to the world—the love that led God to send His only Son to die for our sins.

For God so loved the world that he gave his one and only Son, that whoever believes in him shall not perish but have eternal life. (John 3:16)

We can mirror this love and take it to the world—but only if we are willing to pay the price through prayer and fasting.

Are you ready to pay the price?

Get yourself prepared for all that God has for you. Set your sights on the goal. Look toward the goal "to win the prize."

I press on toward the goal to win the prize for which God has called me heavenward in Christ Jesus. (Philippians 3:14)

Instruct your spirit-man. Let it be known in every part of your body, mind, and soul that you intend to seek God and do His will. Then allow the Lord to do a mighty work in you and through you as you seek Him through prayer and fasting.

Get ready for the many blessings God has in store for you. And be prepared—there are a lot of them. You must only open the floodgates of heaven through earnest prayer and fasting to receive them.

My Prayer
for You

MY PRAYER FOR YOU

Friend, let me ask you: When was the last time you sought the face of God in prayer and fasting? If you are honest, you will recognize that you need God's grace. Let us believe God together as we pray.

Heavenly Father,

I pray that the anointing of the Holy Spirit will rest heavily upon the words of this book. These are Your words. May every word come to rest in my heart. And may I be stirred to action.

Help me to make a commitment to receive what You have spoken and to apply it to everyday life.

Strengthen me! Encourage me! Cause me to rise up as a mighty prepared army that will go forth in Your power.

Give me power to overcome the appetites that endeavor to take control over my spirit life. Give me purpose and direction to follow You from this day forward.

In Jesus' name I pray—and I thank You for the answer,

Amen!

Appendices

A QUICK BIBLE GUIDE TO PRAYER AND FASTING

As we saw in chapter 6, fasting is not some newfangled thing created by man. Fasting is a biblical mandate, and the Bible is filled with examples of godly men and women who regularly practiced prayer and fasting. Here is a guide to some of the instances of fasting in the Bible, as well as the reasons behind those fasts. As you will see, God calls His people to fast for many different purposes.

WHEN TO FAST

IN TIMES OF MOURNING

- Ezra 10:6
- Nehemiah 9:1–2 (for sins)
- Esther 4:1–3 (for decree to kill Jews)
- Esther 9:30–32
- 1 Samuel 31:11–13
- 2 Samuel 1:11–12
- 1 Chronicles 10:11–12
- Psalm 69:10
- Zechariah 7:1–5

WHEN KINGS PRAY AND FAST

WHEN SEEKING GUIDANCE

- Judges 20:23–26
- 2 Chronicles 20:1–4
- Psalm 35:13
- Psalm 109:21–24
- Daniel 9:3
- Acts 13:2–3
- Acts 14:23

FOR HEALING, DELIVERANCE, AND SAFETY

- Isaiah 58:6–7
- Ezra 8:21–23
- Esther 4:16
- 2 Samuel 12:16–23

DURING TIMES OF REPENTANCE

- 1 Kings 21:27–29
- 1 Samuel 7:6
- Nehemiah 1:4–7
- Jeremiah 36:1–9
- Joel 1:1–14
- Joel 2:12–15
- Jonah 3:4–9

WHEN SEEKING THE FACE OF GOD

- Matthew 4:1–2
- Luke 2:36–37

TO SHOW OUR DESIRE FOR THE LORD'S RETURN

- Matthew 9:14–15
- Mark 2:18–20
- Luke 5:33–35

SPIRITUAL RESULTS OF FASTING

FASTING IS A MEANS OF HUMBLING OURSELVES TOWARD GOD

> *Yet when they were ill, I put on sackcloth and humbled myself with fasting.* (Psalm 35:13)

FASTING DISCIPLINES THE BODY AND MAKES IT A USEFUL INSTRUMENT TO GOD

> *No, I beat my body and make it my slave so that after I have preached to others, I myself will not be disqualified for the prize.* (1 Corinthians 9:27)

FASTING DETERMINES OUR VICTORY OVER FLESHLY DESIRES

> *Their destiny is destruction, their god is their stomach, and their glory is in their shame. Their mind is on earthly things.* (Philippians 3:19)

FASTING BUILDS FAITH AND REMOVES HELPLESSNESS IN SOLVING PROBLEMS

> *Howbeit this kind goeth not out but by prayer and fasting.* (Matthew 17:21 KJV)

FASTING OPENS THE DOOR FOR INTIMACY WITH GOD AND BUILDS THE INNER SPIRIT

> *But seek first his kingdom and his righteousness, and all these things will be given to you as well.* (Matthew 6:33)

FASTING CLEARS THE WAY FOR YOU TO HEAR THE VOICE OF GOD

> *You will seek me and find me when you seek me with all your heart.* (Jeremiah 29:13)

FASTING HELPS US INTERCEDE FOR OTHERS

> *At that time I, Daniel, mourned for three weeks. I ate no choice food; no meat or wine touched my lips; and I used no lotions at all until the three weeks were over.* (Daniel 10:2–3)

FOOD AND BEVERAGE GUIDELINES

The most important advice I can give you while you're in the midst of a fast, no matter what kind of fast it is, is to *drink plenty of water*. Here are some other key points to keep in mind, as well. The food guidelines are geared toward those undergoing partial fasts, Daniel fasts, and juice fasts. (See pages 154, 156–157.)

BEVERAGES

- Drink distilled water; it draws toxic wastes out of the body.

- Water should be tepid, not hot or cold.

- Try to drink 8 oz. of water every thirty minutes to an hour.

- For a nice warm drink, try peppermint herbal tea, or add a small amount of apple cider vinegar to warm water.

- Ladies, drink rose hip tea, which is rich in vitamin E. (Vitamin E is essential to metabolism in women.)

- Make sure to read all juice labels. Do not drink anything labeled "concentrate." Drink fresh, unsweetened juices only.

FRUITS AND VEGETABLES

- Use raw vegetables and fruits over cooked ones. They have live enzymes and nutrients that are good for your body.
- If you have a juicer, take advantage of it! Use it to create fresh juices from raw fruits and vegetables.

DAIRY

- If you must have a dairy product during a fast, use diluted plain yogurt, which is good for cleaning the lining of the colon. Other dairy products contain an indigestible enzyme.

FOOD TO AVOID

- Avoid all canned foods.
- Avoid bread, especially bread made with white flour, which becomes like glue in your colon. If you must have bread, opt for whole-grain bread, and use it sparingly.
- Avoid all fried foods.
- Avoid salt.
- Avoid caffeine.
- Avoid sugar.
- Avoid sugar substitutes since even these cause you to crave sweets, making it difficult to maintain your fast.

About
the Author

ABOUT THE AUTHOR

His Royal Majesty KING ADAMTEY I [known in private life as Dr. Kingsley Fletcher] is the SUAPOLOR [the pathfinder and waymaker] for the SE (Shai) people, Kingdom and State, Ghana, West Africa, leading his people beyond the twenty-first century into peace, progress, and prosperity. His life and influence touches millions around the world. His work as a well-known author, humanitarian, historian, respected international advisor, and minister has spanned over one hundred countries covering five continents. Many heads of state and global leaders seek His Majesty for his wisdom and counsel in various areas, including international relations, economic, community, and social development.